I0034515

7 Steps to Entrepreneurial Victory!

The Victory Code to Drive Profits
and Run Your Business at
the Platinum Level

CHRIS VANDERZYDEN

Copyright © 2014 Chris Vanderzyden Global, LLC

To book Chris Vanderzyden for a speaking engagement,
Visit http://chrisvanderzyden.com

All rights reserved. No part of this book may be used or reproduced by any means, graphic, electronic or mechanical, including photocopying, recording, taping or by any information storage retrieval system without the written permission of the publisher, except in the case of brief quotations embodied in critical articles and reviews.

The scanning, uploading and distribution of this book via the Internet or via any other means without the permission of the publisher is illegal and punishable by law. Please purchase only authorized electronic editions and do not participate in or encourage electronic piracy of copyrightable materials. Your support of the author's rights is appreciated.

ISBN: 978-0-9854148-3-2

Library of Congress Cataloging –in– Publication Data has been applied for.

Published by Marie Street Press

5760 Legacy Drive, Suite B3-454, Plano, TX 75024

Tel: 214-519-8033   Web: mariestreetpress.com

Cover Art by Brenda Phelps Shih

Because of the dynamic nature of the Internet, any web addresses or links contained in this book may have changed since publication and may no longer be valid.

The author of this book does not dispense medical advice or prescribe the use of any techniques as a form of treatment for physical, emotional, or medical problems without the advice of a physician, either directly or indirectly. The intent of the author is only to offer information of a general nature to help you in your quest for emotional and spiritual well-being. In the event you use any of the information in this for yourself, which is your constitutional right, the author and the publisher assume no responsibility for your actions.

Printed in the United States of America

"A must read for any entrepreneur, whether you are just beginning your entrepreneurial journey or you've been at it for a long time. You can open this book to any page and find a wealth of helpful guidance and food for thought. The *7 Steps to Entrepreneurial VICTORY* is chock full of practical, actionable advice that is sure to expand your capacity to succeed as an entrepreneur. I highly recommend this book to anyone who wants to take their entrepreneurial pursuit to the next level."

David A. O'Brien,
President of WorkChoice Solutions and
bestselling author of *The Navigator's Handbook,
101 Leadership Lessons for Work & Life*

"Working and consulting for successful companies that were started by entrepreneurs, I have seen Chris's 7 Steps to VICTORY in play. These seven steps are embedded into their everyday thinking and processes; it's what allows them to remain relevant. This is a must read for those looking to start a business or for those searching for answers to move their business to a higher rank."

David E. Otani,
Founder OTANI8: builders and fixers of retail businesses

"Whether you are entering a market as an entrepreneur or already leading an organization in an established sector, *7 Steps to Entrepreneurial VICTORY* offers a compelling roadmap on how to go about driving real business results and beating the competition, systematically."

Jim Young,
President, Davidoff North America and
Vice Chairman of the Board - The BOMA Project

"Chris Vanderzyden has a point to make. Disruption creates opportunity. *7 Steps to Entrepreneurial VICTORY* is your roadmap to identify those opportunities and master them for your own success."

Willis Turner, CAE, CME CSE
President Sales & Marketing Executives International, Inc.

"Thinking about starting your own business, but not sure now is the time? Then Vanderzyden's new book is a must read. Now is the perfect time to launch your entrepreneurial venture and this book gives you the insight, information and inspiration you need to soar to success. Consider Vanderzyden your personal mentor and go make it happen."

Susan Solovic,
THE Small Business Expert, NYT Bestselling author of *It's Your Biz* and award-winning Internet pioneer

"Chris nailed it! A trusted framework entrepreneurs can use to build a flourishing business that matters!"

David Horsager
Founder of Horsager Leadership and
bestselling author of *The Trust Edge*

"As all successful business owners know, while it's the desire to win that brings you to the starting line, it's your preparation, conscious awareness and considerate measured pace that sees you through to victory. Accomplished entrepreneurs, like professional athletes, understand the value of having an actionable game plan to achieve maximum performance. Chris has drawn from her extensive business and personal experiences to create this comprehensive guide to entrepreneurial achievement. How fortunate you will be to have her as your coach on this journey!"

David Fergusson,
President, The M&A Advisor

"As a CPA, I have worked with literally hundreds of clients as they struggle to get their business started or take their business to the next level. I now have a new tool to provide to my clients that will not only save them money, but will be an invaluable resource to them throughout their journey…a copy of Chris' book!"

Michael J. Yuda, CPA/PFS

"Chris Vanderzyden provides and accommodates the 'express lane' to success and ultimate victory by stimulating and facilitating the necessary courage and confidence by matching vision with intent and purpose through her well crafted and insightful methodology and her inspired instincts gained through invaluable experience. Other writers may conduct research on their subject, but Chris has actually lived and continues to live by these learnings and is the shining embodiment of the belief that regardless of our situation, or aspirations, it is how we choose to respond that says everything about us - whether we like it or not!"

Ade Djajamihardja, Australia.
Film and TV Producer, Speaker and Author of
*The Little Book of Hope for Stroke Survivors, Caregivers and
Anyone Else Going Through a Really Shit Time*

"Chris has a deep understanding of how our level of personal development impacts our level of business success. This book gives valuable guidance in driving both from the inside out. A must read for any small business or entrepreneur."

Jacques Bazinet,
InsideOut Development

"This is one great read for the new or budding entrepreneur. In a no-nonsense down to earth and sometimes witty account Chris Vanderzyden has captured in a focused and concise way an almost athletic road map to business success. By following Chris's seven steps your business will make it to the winners' podium - which is where you want to be. This is one well-constructed guide that should never be far from your side."

Dr. Gerard O'Hare CDE DL FRICS

"Entrepreneurs and wantrepreneurs, listen up! Put down that stack of books—Chris Vanderzyden has done the reading and research for you. *7 Steps to Entrepreneurial VICTORY* summarizes **best practices** from the brightest minds in business, combining education and advice from subject matter experts with real-world examples from the author's own experience. An accomplished business owner, tri-athlete and professional coach, Chris has learned what it takes to prepare, compete and win."

Kelly Carmichael,
MissManagement,
Contributor to HuffPo and Good Morning America

"Chris knows firsthand the importance of staying fit and thinking clearly. Both integrate the importance of goal orientation with drive toward the finish. These are compatible short and long term integrated ways of life."

Dr. Richard Davis Hart,
DO FACOS and
Former World Swim Record Holder English Channel (1972)

"If you want to be victorious in your entrepreneurial endeavors, you need Chris Vanderzyden's *7 Steps to Entrepreneurial VICTORY*. No Entrepreneur should be without it by their side, every single day."

Dr. Natalie Petouhoff,
VP and Principle Analyst Constellation Research

"Chris nails the importance of taking action and being your own rainmaker. Her message coupled with solid marketing strategies gives the reader a fail proof guide to creating a steady stream of profitable sales. A must read for every small business searching for a path to growth."

Mark Satterfield,
Founder and CEO of Gentle Rain Marketing Inc

"A new visionary has arrived on the scene who has been able to analyze what makes a business succeed and distill that knowledge into seven simple steps which, if utilized properly will ultimately lead to entrepreneurial success. Chris has provided a road map, which, if followed carefully will result in the achievement of every businessman's goal – a successful and profitable enterprise. The analytical tools she provides allow the seeker to examine and identify his strengths, his weaknesses, his opportunities, and the threats to his success, and, most importantly, deal with them appropriately."

Mercedes Rundle, PsyD

"Entrepreneurship applies to social enterprises too. Chris has provided a book that will guide entrepreneurs to succeed and create lasting impact. Her book is a must read for people who want to elevate their business and bring about positive change."

Kathleen Colson,
CEO bomaproject.org

"Why should you read this book? Chris Vanderzyden is different. CPA in the corporate world, entrepreneur, speaker, author, mum, great friend, and athlete – she has been through all the ups and downs which means she has seen for herself what works! This is a must-read for anyone planning to start a business, and even more so if you have one already and are looking to move it to the next level. In today's world there are so many impulses hitting us every day – TV, radio, Internet, cell phone, Facebook and, and it is hard to understand what will truly make a difference in developing your business. VICTORY distills the necessary information needed to achieve success. Wherever in the world you have your business or plan to have it – all you need to know is in the *7 Steps to Entrepreneurial VICTORY!*"

Kevin Barber,
Executive Director BNI Germany South-West
Creator of BNI® Connect 5

"In the world of social marketing, competition is fierce. Exterior forces will attempt to derail you and drown you out of the conversation. Success comes from knowing your audience, having a clear vision of what they need, planning carefully and exercising the skills necessary to outstrip the competition. This book will help you to develop everything you need for your own business to be successful, regardless of what industry you're in. Take the time to study it, and you're sure to claim Victory!"

Tara R. Alemany,
Owner/Founder of Aleweb Social Marketing,
Inspirational Speaker and Author of *The Best is Yet to Come*

"During the dot.com boom, firms like Salon.com spent over $10m building the infrastructure to run their business. Advances in technology would bring that cost down to $50k today. Entrepreneurs can accomplish significantly more today than they ever could. This along with the changing nature of the workforce will inspire many more entrepreneurs to enter the market. Just because there will be more entrepreneurs with better technology doesn't mean there will be significantly more successes. To be successful in today's fast-paced technology-enabled world, you need to follow a plan to entrepreneurial success. Chris has encapsulated all the necessary information in this book. Read it to help you on your entrepreneurial journey."

Mitchell Levy,
Thought Leader Architect, THiNKaha and author of 21 books including *#Creating Thought Leaders* tweetbook

"Following her inspiring book *A-Z Blueprint For Success*, Vanderzyden now gives her readers a detailed roadmap that shows them everything they'll need for entrepreneurial success. As a professional investor, I've learned to focus on what distinguishes a great business from all the others, the factors that create lasting profitability and business quality. Similarly, Chris describes the keys to business success by explaining how to create value for your customers and distinguish yourself from your competition. Using the metaphor of athletic competition (triathlon), she shows how the self-discipline, strategies, and motivation of an athlete can provide a model for the aspiring entrepreneur. And just like a successful athlete with a great plan, the business owner using Chris's book will be well on their way toward victory in the marketplace. As someone who got an MBA and now runs their own business, I say skip the MBA and buy this book."

Dan Hutner,
President, Hutner Capital Management

"Chris hits in on the head with *7 Steps to Entrepreneurial VICTORY*. The combination of motivation pertaining to small businesses and the blueprint on how to do it is an inspiration"

Danny Friedman,
Vice President, Added Incentive, Inc.

"When reading 7 *Steps to Entrepreneurial VICTORY*, I felt like I was talking to Chris directly – it POPS – just like Chris does! This is a great read but also something to go back to time and time again. Follow the Pillars and you will be well on your way to success."

Thea Kelly,
NYC Marathoner and CPA

"Chris gives a step-by-step plan for entrepreneurial success in a format and style that's easy to use. A great book for any entrepreneur's bookshelf!"

Troy Harrison,
Author of *Sell Like Your Mean It*

"Unlike many strategic business books, Chris incorporates a key element that many entrepreneurs fail to identify and that is to align your core values to your vision. She explores the impact of this combination which can truly make the difference between becoming disengaged and the "victory" of loving the life AND business you create. What an excellent guide for new business owners to embrace!"

Nancy West,
CEO, Accelerated Performance, Inc. and
Author of *What Are You Waiting For? You Don't Have Nine Lives*

"Starting a business and growing it successfully means paying attention to the holistic process of learning about the customers in the market, recognizing the opportunities in the larger system of partnerships and supply chain, and adapting the capabilities of the business to mature and scale. Chris has brought all of this together in this book with a mindset for sustainable growth. And she takes it above and beyond with a rigor and discipline for using marketing metrics to revise strategy and ensure that marketing drives bottom line results. In short, this is a roadmap that will help you on your entrepreneurial journey."

Kate O'Neill,
Founder and CEO of KO Insights and
startup mentor and advisor

"The *7 Steps to Entrepreneurial VICTORY* provides great insightful, actionable truths about entrepreneurship and building a business. I work with leaders every day who are in the business of providing services, but forget about the challenge of building great teams. The challenge of finding and building teams of people who are as committed and passionate about your business is one of the biggest challenges that businesses face as they grow. In *7 Steps to Entrepreneurial VICTORY*, Chris knows that developing a great team is not only a good thing, but what can launch your business a head of the pack!"

Kerri Tietgen,
KT Consulting, Inc.

"In my thirty plus years of consulting to boards and senior management of global businesses, the one component which makes the difference between good and great companies is that great companies develop their future leadership beginning in the early years of their tenure. Chris' book highlights the importance of great leadership and its impact on success. Be a leader and read it today!"

Steven Dear,
President, Global Leadership Consulting, Inc.

"Chris is a master at guiding her entrepreneurial reader to victory. Her words simplify the process by making it so real and so achievable. Follow her practicable words of wisdom and she will help that journey doable."

Joyce Buford,
Producer and Host of SecondWind on Toginet Radio

"This is a HOLISTIC guide to creating and then growing a successful business. Chris not only has the business acumen and experience that will help you to create a profitable business from a financial stand point, she also has the life skills that will help both you and your business to flourish and ensure a balanced life and emotional fulfillment. As you read Chris's book it becomes very obvious that she loves teaching and helping others to succeed. I have been very fortunate to also experience Chris's authentic care and her superior business skills as a Victory coaching client."

Kate Stephens, Australia

"Chris provides telling and penetrating insights into the process of starting a successful business. She captures the continuous challenge of balancing Big Picture goals and objectives with the high attention to detail every entrepreneur needs to steer his/her new venture straight and true within the ever-changing and ever-evolving seascape of the global environment."

David Chandler,
Partner Chandler 4 Corners and
The BOMA Project Chairman

"Being an entrepreneur and a triathlete, I was immediately drawn in by Chris Vanderzyden's compelling yet approachable book about being successful in business. Her description of swimming in open water and the need to stay on course is a wonderful analogy for developing and following a compelling vision. Further, the chapter titled Review, Revise & Re-do presents practical (and needed) guidance both for people starting out in business and those trying to grow existing businesses."

Darryl Rosen,
Bestselling author of *See You at the Finish Line*

"As a small business owner, Chris provides the right insights that will resonate with any entrepreneur looking to take their business to the next level. From the mind shift of embracing change and the challenge of managing growth in a smart way, this book provides all the tools that entrepreneurs need to guarantee long-term success."

Ana Rahona,
Co-Founder of L&R Communications

To all the brave entrepreneurs
who believe they can achieve

The VICTORY Code

A few guidelines as to how I have organized this book: The VICTORY Code is a comprehensive program and is broken into three sections that cover seven key concepts that create a successful business.

Since I believe the degree of physical and emotional care you provide yourself impacts the success of your business, and since I have been a runner my entire life, the three sections are divided into Pre-Race, Race Day, and Post-Race segments. Each part of the race is important, and ultimately the success you create in your business will be determined by your willingness to take action.

Contents

Foreword by Jeffrey Hayzlett

The ability to respond to change will dictate a business's success or failure. And it isn't just responding to change that matters, but also how the organization responds, and when. Is the company proactive or reactive?

I believe most leaders and employees know when their old ways of doing business must change or their business will die; yet they don't act. They have the ability to enact big changes, but too often they just don't. Maybe they can't see what needs to be done. Maybe they are scared of mistakes or failure. Maybe they refuse to hold themselves accountable and take responsibility. Maybe change seems too hard, and they are too tired. But change won't ever come passively through attrition, delegation or waiting around for someone else to take responsibility.

So, how do you learn to act like an agent of change? The same way I do; you get up in your business. If it isn't working, change it and own those changes. Refuse to tolerate problems and passivity. Period.

My book *Running the Gauntlet* defines the importance of acknowledging the forces of change and taking decisive action in driving the success of a business. (Find Jeff's book online at chrisvanderzyden.com/RunningTheGauntlet.)

Change is inevitable, and the *7 Steps to Entrepreneurial Victory* speaks my language. Chris inspires her readers to recognize the forces of change, harness the energy of innovation, and capitalize on the opportunities change presents by entering the world of entrepreneurship.

But, people fail. Businesses fail. And entrepreneurs… fail in great numbers. Read this book, follow the steps and avoid failure.

The list of reasons for failure is as long as the prairie stretches on. For most, they simply don't have the knowledge or the tools to create success in a business. Life as an entrepreneur is very much like running the gauntlet, requiring a small business owner to not only be agile in the face of change, but to be very adept in the multitude of functions necessary to run a successful business.

Chris's *7 Steps to Entrepreneurial Victory* is the antidote to failure. Her seven-step comprehensive code is an all-encompassing program to ensure every function of a business is contributing to its profitability and the business continues to run at the platinum level.

She doesn't sugarcoat the process of creating a business, and she guides her reader through self-discovery to assess if the entrepreneurial world is the right rodeo for him or her.

She prods the reader to take a long, hard look to discern if his or her business model can withstand the force of competition. She challenges the review of every aspect of the business to ensure all strategies and tactics are in line with producing a profitable business. She further explores how to identify the obstacles that can prohibit the achievement of success and offers up clear strategies to overcome those obstacles.

Chris clearly likes to win.

With real-world experience as a CPA and as an entrepreneur, Chris is a champion for all entrepreneurs. If you want to ensure your business is a success, read this book, take action, implement the strategies, and make Chris part of your winning team.

Jeffrey Hayzlett

Bestselling Author and
Host of Bloomberg *Television's C-Suite with Jeffrey Hayzlett*

The Journey into Entrepreneurship Begins

I WAS THIRTY-FOUR YEARS OLD when I began my journey as an entrepreneur. And, like many, it wasn't a completely planned adventure. But how many of us actually land where we intend?

My career began in the mid-eighties, fresh out of college with an accounting and economics degree in hand, with Coopers & Lybrand, now known as PricewaterhouseCoopers. I was first an auditor, gaining experience to earn my CPA, and then became a real estate tax specialist.

I played in the corporate arena for twelve years in Los Angeles first as a CPA, and at the end of my tenure, as a real estate asset manager.

My twelve years in Los Angeles were exciting and, at the same time, daunting. I found the corporate structure to be incredibly constraining and, at the time, women were still not treated equally.

At one point in my career, I was overseeing 1.2 million square feet of office space and was certified as a CPA and RPA, but was making one-third less than a male colleague of mine who had no certifications and half the square footage of responsibility.

The archaic corporate culture became increasingly frustrating, unbearable, and the chaos of Los Angeles no longer enticing, as I yearned for a quieter pace.

I became pregnant with my first child in 1996 and quickly recognized that my corporate path was not going to be conducive to living the balanced life that I craved with a family.

Surprising to my colleagues, I jumped off the corporate treadmill and landed in a small town in Vermont.

I was officially a corporate defector.

That transition is for an entirely separate book; however, I will say that after having lived in a cosmopolitan area and in the corporate world for over a decade, life in Vermont with no career was…quiet.

I felt like I was living out the 1980s movie *Baby Boom*, starring Diane Keaton. I enjoyed the life-balance I was able to achieve but was desperately craving the stimulation that a career provides.

When I left Los Angeles, the partners in the asset management company I had left behind couldn't believe that I had jilted my career just as we were heading for the altar of partnership.

So, after I had been in Vermont for about six months, in an attempt to lure me back, they called offering me a project in Washington, D.C. Well, I was ready to pack up and leave the quiet life. Six months was enough for me, thank you very much. But my husband was adamant that he was not leaving Vermont. Hmm… Fine.

My answer to the exceedingly deafening quiet of Vermont was, of course, entrepreneurship. Like many people before me, it took a few false starts to figure out what my new business would be.

I entertained forming a real estate company, a property management group and, at one time, drowning in maternal hormones, an infant apparel business. I still remember the very cute prototype infant hat I had produced!

Eventually I went back to my roots and began doing financial and business consulting. I was a solopreneur, controlling my work schedule and making a decent living.

This worked well for several years while I gave birth to my second child and laid the foundation for my family life. Very quickly however, I grew restless.

I then identified a gap in the market and created an advertising specialty business. Thanks to the Internet, I was able to grow this business to become a nationwide company that produced millions of dollars of revenue. I was then truly an entrepreneur with a scalable venture.

Entrepreneurship was a perfect fit for me. I loved the autonomy and ability to create a business with no boundaries. I could make as much money as I wanted and I had complete control over my time. This brought ease and fulfillment to my life as I brought up my family.

This success, however, did not come without failures, I assure you. There were many challenges along the way. The umbrella of the corporate structure allows you to be very focused upon your individual skill, and there is safety in the fact that your success is dependent only upon your performance in one particular area.

As an entrepreneur, however, you suddenly need to be very adept at all the skills necessary to run a business.

I remember the first time I had a technological challenge as I was struggling to pull together a presentation that was due in an hour. What? No tech guy down the hall? Yikes. Technology issues always send me to the highest level of frustration possible.

Figuring out how to do it "all" was no picnic. I always felt that with each challenge there must be an easier way, but what? How?

This is why I have written The VICTORY Code;
to forge an easier path to success for small businesses.

Now, as I sit here in Vermont almost twenty years later I recognize that despite the frustrations of developing my own business, entrepreneurship was the vehicle that has provided me with exactly the kind of life that I wanted and have today; balanced, fulfilling both financially and emotionally, and with a greater sense of ease about my future.

Entrepreneurship is not the right road for everyone, but if it is what you desire, and if you strive to acquire the knowledge needed and take action, success can be yours.

From Main Street establishments to high-tech startups, now is the perfect time to launch your business, follow your dreams and become an entrepreneur.

Never before in our economic history has the business climate been so keenly conducive to creating a successful business. Whether you are a start-up or a small business seeking to shift to a higher level, today is a great day to take action, leverage the abundance of resources available and elevate your business.

If you need convincing, here are the top seven reasons why now is the time to enter the world of owning your own business:

1. **Technology** – Cloud-based technology has reduced the cost of starting a business significantly. Investment in technology was once a very expensive requirement of starting a business. Now it is available on demand and no longer requires the financial commitment it once did.

2. **Political disruption** – Increasing change in not only technology but also in regulations has created a dynamic environment in which opportunities to develop and fill market gaps are plentiful.

3. **Globalization** – Thanks to increased communication, our world has created an economy where commerce on a worldwide basis can easily be enjoyed.

4. **Funding** –The availability of capital from non-traditional resources, such as crowdfunding, has created new space for entrepreneurs and small business owners to raise the necessary funds for start-up and growth.

5. **Support** – The availability of knowledge through mentors and coaches has leveled the playing field and

paved the way to create a successful business quicker than ever.

6. **Ease of connection** – Networking opportunities, such as LinkedIn, have created a plethora of communities available to support businesses.

7. **Ability to outsource processes** – It used to be that you needed to hire an entire crew to build a successful business. Now we can outsource many aspects of a business, which creates efficiencies and saves time and money.

According to the Kauffman Index of Entrepreneurial Activity, a leading new business indicator, over 540,000 businesses are launched each month.

Businesses are being created at an unprecedented rate for a myriad of reasons. Since the days when I was a CPA, there has been a tremendous shift in the corporate world. The formula at one time was: you went to college, studied hard, got a great job with a company, and stayed with that company until you cashed in on your defined benefit pension plan.

Times have changed, and the security we once relied on in the corporate structure is an old paradigm. In its place, people have become inspired to take control and create stability and success for themselves by owning their own businesses.

Unfortunately, the failure rate of new businesses, according to the Harvard Business School, hovers at about 75% within the first five years.

The top five reasons businesses fail within the first five years are:

1. Presenting no real differentiation in the market, meaning the business lacks a unique value proposition to fill a gap.
2. Failure to effectively communicate the value proposition clearly, concisely and in a way so compelling that your target market not only notices you, but also takes action and engages you.
3. Failure of the leaders to engage in personal development and perform at their top level.
4. Failure to plan, test, create and sustain a profitable business model.
5. Not effectively engaging with target audiences and understanding their needs as they change and expand.

Within this book we will address all of these top failure points.

Now, there are many amazingly successful entrepreneurs, so beyond tools and knowledge, let's review a few common traits and habits that these business owners share:

- Successful entrepreneurs have high character qualities. They are positive, disciplined and hold a mindset of success. They are resilient and agile in their response to challenges, and they also have a clear vision of what they want to achieve.
- The owners have taken the time to create a blueprint to guide them to their success. This means they have

created a rock solid business plan, goals, and the strategies and tactics to support those goals.

- They take continuous action and are passionate about what they "do." They have created an organizational structure and processes that run smoothly and create efficiencies, ensuring the highest level of productivity.

- They have created systems that allow them to work *on* their business, not always *in* their business. This provides them the opportunity to creatively overcome any obstacles to their success and more effectively identify growth opportunities.

- Lastly, and possibly most important, successful entrepreneurs never let fear get in the way of taking action. They utilize fear to make proper assessments and then they take a calculated risk.

If you possess the above characteristics of a successful entrepreneur, take action, utilize the information provided in this book and leverage the economic conditions present today, your ability to create an enormously successful business is there for the taking.

Since the Harvard Business School estimates that 75% of businesses fail within the first five-years, let's talk briefly about failure.

If you feel that you are failing in your business, or perhaps have experienced a colossal failure in your past, you are in great company.

Many entrepreneurs have failed prior to creating huge success in their businesses. Failures are merely stepping-stones to success and, as long as you fail quickly, learn even quicker from your mistakes and apply your new lessons, you will achieve what you desire in your business.

I encourage all entrepreneurs to fail in an epic way and learn from their mistakes. Personally, my success happened when I hit the peak of failure.

A great example of failure and the rising of success was Steve Jobs.

Steve Jobs experienced great failure on his path to success. Jobs was also one of our greatest visionaries. He wanted to change the world and he succeeded; however, he also had a few failures along the way.

He began his amazing contributions to the technological age with the formation of Apple Computer with co-founder Steve Wozniak. With its initial success, Apple went public in 1980.

John Sculley, who was recruited from Pepsi-Cola by Steve Jobs, then became CEO of Apple. The focus immediately began to shift from creating great products to generating great profits.

Under Sculley's direction the tide began to turn, and with the sluggish sales of the "Lisa" computer (the only reason anyone would remember this computer is because it was named after Jobs' daughter) and incessant quality control issues, Jobs was fired by Sculley in 1985.

Jobs then started NeXT Computer, a hardware and software company, which focused on mass marketing its specialized operating system. In time, NeXT proved itself to be a dismal failure, and its only success was that Apple eventually purchased NeXT's software division. Apple's purchase of NeXT opened the channel for Jobs' return to Apple as CEO in 1997.

Steve Jobs famously acknowledged that his big failure at Apple was allowing profits to be the main focus and not his passion for the work.

Upon his return as CEO in 1997, Jobs focused on passion, creativity and innovation of new products and drove Apple to new heights realizing his ultimate success and, in fact, changing our world.

And then there are the "common" folk who struggle to create a profitable business. You know the people. The dry cleaner who wasn't quite sure how to compete with the new dry cleaner with a seamstress and at-your-door full service who opened up a quarter mile down the street, or the sales rep who is functioning in a hyper-competitive commoditized market and unsure of how to differentiate his business from the competition, or the accounting firm that is struggling to acquire new clients as their older clientele transition away, or the dentist who isn't quite sure why revenue doesn't match his production level (hint: employee theft), or how about the employee who woke up one day at the top of her career only to discover that her ladder was leaning against the wrong wall and now is struggling to pave the way as an entrepreneur and overwhelmed by the process of creating a profitable business.

There are many reasons businesses fail. Most failures hinge on a lack of knowledge—knowing what to do, when to do it and how to do it—and ultimately on not taking action. Sometimes, it is due to a lack of passion to pursue a vision with undying enthusiasm.

Most new entrepreneurs, quite frankly, get scared. They aren't willing to be open to new ideas. They don't take appropriate action and refuse to try new methods. They are not willing to be honest and assess the current state of their business. They possess negative attitudes and have these little voices inside their heads telling them they can't, shouldn't, don't deserve, blah blah blah.

And, worse yet, they actually pay attention to those little voices. They don't take the time to acquire new knowledge and, more importantly, implement the new knowledge. They aren't willing to invest in themselves or their business. They have tunnel vision and can't see all that is possible. That is failure in a nutshell.

As mentioned previously, the challenge most small business owners face is that in order to be successful, they must be adept in all the disciplines of running a business.

Most individuals come from the corporate world with a specific expertise that is focused in one particular area, whether it is marketing, finance, sales, technology or other core functions of an organization. This focus upon one specialized area does not lend itself to success as a small business owner—it takes becoming a multi-disciplined expert.

This is why I wrote this book. *The VICTORY Code* will serve as the antidote to failure.

The challenges of running a small business are broad, but the opportunity to create wealth, ease and fulfillment in your life is the ultimate driving force behind the all-time high introduction rate of new businesses.

The VICTORY Code will provide the knowledge, tools and inspiration required to ensure that your business is a huge success. It will teach you to create a blueprint to be used as a guide, to create the success in your business that you deserve and desire.

In this information era we are bombarded with "solutions," but discerning what methods, "secrets," techniques and tools will truly have a positive impact on your business is a job in itself.

The VICTORY Code is a comprehensive guide of tried-and-true actions that ensure that entrepreneurs and small business owners create a profitable business.

The Code will relieve the frustration of knowing the appropriate steps to take in order to drive profits in your business; it will take away the guesswork and provide you with a course of action that will create a profitable business.

Follow these seven steps and you will attain VICTORY and create an enduringly successful business. (Note that "victory" is an acronym for the seven steps.)

Section I – Pre-Race

The planning that takes place before a business is launched goes a long way to ensure the business becomes a success.

Understanding the vision, the competitive market, why the business will attract customers, and testing the plan is important. Don't breeze through this section, as taking the time to plan can save time and dollars in mistakes later.

Chapter 1. Vision Matters: Defog Your Goggles

Success begins with having a clear vision of the purpose for the existence of the business.

This chapter is devoted to creating a crystal clear vision that is aligned with your core values and is the foundation for creating a blueprint to building a successful business.

Chapter 2. Identify the Gap in the Game and Start Planning

Passion for the sport, the product, the service does not make a medalist. A product or service must fill a gap in the market in order to have a competitive edge on game day.

In this chapter, we assess the value proposition, review the business model and take steps toward creating a business plan. We'll also discuss how to create an impact with your elevator pitch so that your message is delivered in a compelling fashion that attracts customers to your door.

Section II – Race Day

At this stage in the game, the planning is in process and the vision and viability of the business established.

Upon race day, as a business readies to launch, all systems and processes are put into place. Leadership capabilities and time management need to be at the highest level in order to turn obstacles into opportunities.

Section II will ready the business for launch and elevate the owner's skill to ensure resilience in the face of challenge.

Chapter 3. Creating the Strategies and Tactics to Win

Explores the seven pillars of a successful business and provides guidance to create a strategic plan of action for operations, marketing, sales, customer service, finance, team development and technology.

Chapter 4. Take Action and Be the Leader of Your Success

Addresses the process of being a leader, achieving goals and becoming the master of your time in order to function at peak performance.

Chapter 5. Converting Obstacles into Opportunities

Provides specific tools to overcome external as well as internal obstacles to ensure that every obstacle is turned into an opportunity.

Section III – Post-Race

Once the race has begun and the business is at full tilt, avoiding complacency is a must—no sitting on one's laurels. This is not the time to coast.

A process of consistently reviewing the strengths and weakness of each pillar will inspire the necessary changes to guarantee that the business continues to grow.

In addition, this section discusses the power of networking and developing a positive tribe of influencers who will function as a guide to growth.

Chapter 6. Review, Revise, Re-Do

Discusses key performance indicators, accountability, and presents very simple tools to ensure that you create sustained success in your business and institute a strategy for continued growth.

Chapter 7. Hanging with the Yeasayers

Explains the importance of hanging out with the yeasayers and the impact of developing a tribe that will assist you in reaching your success.

As a bonus I have also brought in a few leading experts as contributors:

Shep Hyken is a customer service and experience expert and a *New York Times* and *Wall Street Journal* bestselling author. He provides key insights into what constitutes great customer service and the impact amazing customer service has on how profitable businesses are.

Joy Murphy is a branding expert, and she drills down on how to create a powerful brand position and will discuss consistent brand engagement.

Kurt Shaver is a LinkedIn expert and provides expert guidance as to how to benefit from this social media vehicle and how to utilize this channel as a selling tool.

Chris Westfall is the author of *The NEW Elevator Pitch*, and is co-creator of The 118 Pitch course with Jeffrey Hayzlett. Chris gives guidance as to how to make a pitch that is compelling and drives action from prospects and all stakeholders in an organization.

Read and enjoy The Code. Create a plan, take action and implement your strategies and tactics, and you will create a successful business. ***And, remember, with the right tools, knowledge and action...success is easy.***

Pre-Race: Training to Launch Your Business

SCAN TO VIEW PRE-RACE VIDEO

chrisvanderzyden.com/victory

*Scan this Quick Response (QR) code and watch the video
that will introduce you to the concepts in the
Pre-Race section of The VICTORY Code.*

How do you use a QR code?

If you have a smartphone, you can use these codes quite easily. All you have to do is download a QR code scanning app from your device's app store, open it and use the app to take a picture of the code. It'll decode the QR code and bring you to our video page.

Here is a list of good QR code scanners for each of the major mobile operating systems:

Android – Google Goggles

Blackberry – Free QR Code Scanner Pro

iOS (iPhone/iPad/iPod Touch) – Google Goggles

Windows Phone – QR Code Reader

Again, once you have the app, simply open it on your phone and it should have a scan option that will look like you are looking through your device's camera. Simply aim at a QR code and scan.

Chapter 1. Vision Matters: Defog Your Goggles

EVERYONE IS GATHERED in the dark, waiting for the first peeps of light, assessing in our minds how ready we are to launch. We have planned for success, practiced, created strategies, and we have summed up our competition. The water is as black as ink, and as the sun emerges, sparkles bounce off the water with promise—a promise to remain calm and for the current to move just right.

The gun goes off. Resembling seals in our shiny black wetsuits, we dive in with the hope to win, or simply enjoy, and some of us to survive. The first stroke is always the hardest, as we silently tell ourselves to settle. Settle our breath, find our rhythm, and remember we have prepared for this.

The field is crowded, the competition intense. The current threatens to push you off course. Focus is the name of the game as you try to remember to pick your head up every 10 strokes in an effort to keep your eye on the buoy—eye on the prize—to stay on course.

The goal is to swim point-to-point and not lose precious time zigzagging your way to the finish. The truth is that as you swim with each stroke someone is elbowing and needling you to move over in an attempt to put you out of business.

Your competition swims over your back and you think, "Will I drown?" That little panic voice of self-doubt: "Did I prepare enough?" Then your mantra: "Be a shark, swim or die."

With each turn of your head, rising so slightly to breathe, another competitor is inches from your face, imitating you. Someone kicks your goggles ajar from your face. They immediately fog and force you to stop and clear your vision.

The current provides a steady exterior force that reminds you there will always be forces that will attempt to derail your success.

By the first buoy you have established your rhythm, you have settled into your zone of competition. Now the trick is to not become complacent as you move towards the final two buoys before moving on to the next phase of competition.

Stroke, pull, head up to watch the line, ignore the swimmers that are kicking in your face, elbowing your head, grabbing at your feet. Keep your focus and maintain your determination that you will beat your competition, you will remain agile, and you will overcome the outside forces.

You can win...whatever that means to you!

That is the start of a triathlon. Much like launching or running a business, there is the need to prepare.

Success doesn't just happen, but is the result of having a clear vision, careful planning and exercising the muscles that build a successful business. It's all in the preparation.

"By failing to prepare, you are preparing to fail."

~ Ben Franklin

So how do we prepare to win?

Just like training for a triathlon, it all begins with having a vision of what we want to accomplish. What is the goal? What does your success look like? Is it to win? To enjoy the ride? Is it to survive or thrive?

In this chapter, we are going to clear up your vision and establish what level of entrepreneurship is in alignment with your core values. We'll also uncover if entrepreneurship is a match for you based on your personality traits.

And in order to make a smooth transition into the entrepreneurial world, we'll do a reality check as to how and when to transform from corporate defector to small business owner.

Let's begin the pre-race preparation…

Defog Your Goggles and Clear Up Your Vision

The most brilliant and successful people in business were great visionaries.

Henry Ford – Henry Ford was one of the all-time greatest visionary entrepreneurs.

*His vision was to create an automobile that
every American could afford.*

He began his career as an engineer for the Edison Illuminating Co., and that experience ignited his passion to become part of the future of a mobile society.

His first invention, a quadricycle, consisted of two attached bicycles powered by a gasoline engine.

This first rendition of an automobile was crude at best. In time, however, he attracted investors and formed Ford Motor Co in 1903 and developed the Model A, an expensive automobile that confined sales unfortunately only to the wealthy.

He did meet his vision of producing an automobile that every American could afford with the Model T. However, with the Model T's attractive price, demand grew to a point that was not sustainable with the current manufacturing process.

In order to fulfill his vision, Henry Ford had to develop a system to produce the automobile in a much more efficient manner, and thus the assembly line was born.

As we all know, the concept of the assembly line changed American manufacturing and began the Industrial Revolution. Henry Ford's clear vision drove him to achieve not only the success of creating an automobile to serve the masses, but he also transformed the American manufacturing process.

Another great visionary: The pink Cadillac lady, Mary Kay Ash.

Mary Kay Ash – Mary Kay Ash was a powerful force in the movement to empower women as entrepreneurs.

Her vision was to create a company where working mothers could work independently, choose the amount of money they wanted to make, and the level of success they wanted to achieve.

Her experience was not unlike many women today. She experienced the glass ceiling and watched men be unfairly promoted ahead of her and so she simply chose to create an organization that would benefit women—a direct-sales cosmetics company.

There were many challenges along the way that threatened to derail her from achieving her vision. A month before the company launched, her husband suddenly died of a heart attack. Her lawyer and her accountant both suggested that she abandon her plan because her husband was pivotal in the financial matters of the business. (I'm betting they were men!)

Mary Kay, however, forged ahead. Her persistence and vision paid off. Mary Kay Cosmetics, Inc. today produces over $2 billion dollars worldwide via independent beauty consultants.

Henry Ford and Mary Kay Ash both had very clear visions of what it was they wanted to achieve and why they wanted to achieve it. **Learning from these very successful predecessors: if there is no vision, then there is no direction, and your success will be at the mercy of the winds.**

Many people are unwilling to envision the possibility of what can be, and remain complacent in their life and business, never choosing to take action or to win.

Success or failure is a choice. Swim or die—it's all a choice.

Success as an entrepreneur requires that you be astutely aware of who you are, have a clearly defined set of core values and a vision that is in alignment with those core values–a vision that is so crystal clear and resonates so deeply with your core values that you are motivated to drive that vision of your future into the present through all obstacles.

Understanding Your Core Values

The first step in creating your vision of a successful business is to understand what motivates you and why you are compelled to choose the entrepreneurial path. Your core values are your key motivators and provide guidance as you make choices and take action in your life.

How well your core values are in alignment with your life choices will dictate your success or failure. For example, if your core values are in conflict with your professional desires, this can set you up for failure, or at the very least feel like a heavy weight on your shoulders as you engage in a business that doesn't match your values.

Your core values serve as the building blocks to creating your vision. What is your vision for your life personally and professionally?

Your personal and professional lives are two pieces of the success puzzle that need to fit together in order for you to be truly successful.

All too often we hear about the very successful business professional who has a train wreck in their personal life. The entrepreneur who is working too many hours (working hard, but not necessarily smart) while the family comes apart. The restaurateur who has a young family but didn't think about the negative impact that being away at night may have on the harmony of home.

There is a cost with every success, however this cost can be minimized if we are making decisions that are in alignment with our core values and our vision is clear.

Most people don't take the time to understand their values and then wonder why their life is conflicted and success so difficult to achieve. When your core values are in alignment with your professional life, there is a sense of ease, everything seems to fit correctly and success comes easily.

For example, in addition to my core value of family, two of my core values are:

Communication – I like communication. I like the written and the spoken word. This is why I became a writer, speaker and educator. It is also important for me to do business with people who are clear communicators. I make choices in my personal relationships based on communication styles. So, if I feel that communication is unclear or there are hidden agendas, I feel there is potential for dishonesty and I will readily edit these people out of my business or personal stream.

Innovation – I really thrive in a changing environment. I like progress. I like new ideas, new thoughts, new people and new places. So my decisions frequently embrace new concepts and a bit of instability—after all I am an entrepreneur. Now if my world were focused on stability and stagnation, for instance when I was a CPA, that would not be a good fit for me. My value for innovation drove me to choose entrepreneurship.

In its simplest form, your core values are your internal compass that will let you know if you are going off course.

Once you have articulated your core values you will find that your decision-making process and success will be easy as you align each decision with your core values.

Appendix A in the back of this book will serve as a guide to help you assess and identify your core values.

Once your core values are clear, ask yourself the following questions and begin creating your personal vision:

1. What are your dreams?
2. What would make your life and your business great?
3. As you move through your day, which interactions feel good and which don't?
4. What isn't working?

The answers to these questions will guide you to define your personal vision of success and to assess if your reality today is meeting your definition.

Take the time to do the exercise in Appendix A and define your core values. Write a vision of what you want your personal and professional life to be like based on your core values.

And while you are writing the detail of your vision, hush any inner voice that tells you that you can't, shouldn't or don't deserve your vision. Go big and create a clear vision of your success.

Then evaluate how your reality today matches up with your vision. Will entrepreneurship be the vehicle to fill your gap?

Now that you have created a vision for your personal life in accordance with your core values, we can begin to create your vision of a successful business and recognize how that integrates into your personal life.

Before we get to the blueprint of developing your business, let's explore the various degrees of entrepreneurship and determine if you possess the traits that contribute to becoming a successful business owner.

What Level of Entrepreneurship?

Based upon your vision for your personal life, what level of entrepreneurship are you seeking?

A *solopreneur* is exactly as it sounds; someone who works alone. Most businesses begin at the level of a solopreneur.

When we first branch out on our own, most of us are cash-strapped and so the business is developed by one singular person who wears all of the hats; chief executive officer, chief marketing officer, chief financial officer, chief problem-solver etc.! Yes, a solopreneur does all the work and keeps all of the profits, and there are no employees. Your income level will be limited by how much you personally can produce in the time allowed.

Most people who choose to be a solopreneur do so because they are driven by their personal vision of lifestyle. They like the autonomy of being able to completely control their destiny and they build a business around what they love to do.

When I started my first business my vision was to work only six hours per day, as I had an infant and this is what worked for me at that time in my life. It spoke to my core value of family and solopreneurship was the answer to controlling my time.

If you choose to expand your business beyond solopreneurship, hire people and focus on increasing market share then you have officially become an **entrepreneur**.

When you begin to scale or grow your business, you have created a different business model that drives you to fill market voids, and your income level is not restricted by what you personally can produce. As an entrepreneur you build a system and a team that creates a sustainable business.

I gauge a successful business that has been scaled by assessing if the owner can walk away from the business for a month and it still runs and produces in his or her absence.

If a business owner can leave unencumbered for a period of time then he or she has set up the systems and processes to support a self-sustaining operation. A true entrepreneurial enterprise then exists.

Do You Have the Muscle to Succeed?

Whether you are a solopreneur or an entrepreneur, successful business owners on the outside always seem to make it all look so easy.

The reality is that the successful business owners who make it look effortless have chosen a business that is in alignment with their core values and they have the "goods" to deliver.

So what do I mean by the goods? Successful business owners share key traits that make them successful. Review the list below and assess whether you have the "goods" and if entrepreneurship is right for you.

1. **Motivation** – Successful entrepreneurs have a high degree of motivation that is emotionally driven and resonates with their core values. It is necessary to be sure that the motivation behind wanting to be a business owner is actually a motivation that will take you the distance through the rough spots. For instance, leaving a crazy boss is not a good enough reason to strike out on your own, hang up a shingle and start a business.

   When you have your own business you will then have 1,000 bosses with the following titles: customers, employees, investors, government agencies, etc., and trust me, a few are bound to be crazy.

   The key motivating factor to drive you to take the risk—and believe me all new businesses are risky—and enter the world of entrepreneurship must be so compelling that you are willing to live, eat, breath and dream your business, especially in the beginning.

   Thinking you will be able to work by yourself, be your own boss, get rich quick and have more free time is a fantasy. Do yourself a favor and honestly assess the motivating force behind your thought to start a business. Which brings me to number two…

2. **Work Ethic** – Successful business owners are self-starters, very passionate about their business and are willing to do whatever it takes to achieve success. Their work ethic does not wane—ever. They are ambitious and

determined. I don't mean run of the mill "I am excited about xyz"—these people teeter on the brink of being obsessive. They feel, smell, taste and dream their business.

The New York Times published a great article entitled "Just Manic Enough: Seeking Perfect Entrepreneurs." This article lays out what a venture capitalist is seeking in the persona of a promising entrepreneur. It turns out that venture capitalists are not only looking for ambition but a slightly hypomania temperament!

I don't believe you have to be slightly unhinged to gain a venture capitalist's attention, but I think the article makes a great point that really successful people are a bit manic in pursuit of their vision.

Do you have the drive that will be required to push through every obstacle in pursuit of your dream?

3. **Positive Attitude –** A positive attitude goes a long way towards building a successful business. Those who possess a naturally positive attitude have an uncanny ability to rebuff what I call the "dream stealers," those people who are relentless in trying to enforce their negativity upon you and convince you that your business will fail.

   Successful entrepreneurs work hard to protect their attitude by surrounding themselves with positive people and instituting a resilient reaction in the face of challenges. They are naturally creative in formulating strategies to overcome every difficulty.

4. **Planners** – Successful entrepreneurs are great visionaries and they take the time to plan for their success. They

understand that creating a plan for their business is imperative and continue to revise their plan as necessary on a systematic basis. They don't stop planning ever. They are always aware of their market and the changing dynamics. They are proactive in their planning process and hyper-aware of the unfolding of opportunities. This affords them the ability to capitalize on any difficulty presented.

5. **Leaders** – Successful business owners are comfortable working by themselves but enjoy working with people. They are natural leaders and understand that business ownership is a team sport. They are able to develop a committed team and understand that the success of the business is dependent upon the success of the individuals.

6. **Continuously Invest in their Development** – The top entrepreneurs have an insatiable appetite for learning. They read magazines, books, industry publications, etc. in an effort to continuously develop their knowledge. They attend workshops, seminars and networking events to heighten their exposure and to further master new skills. They understand that information and technology is forever changing and their success is dependent upon their ability to embrace new ideas and implement new strategies that create efficiencies and new paths to profits.

7. **Risk-Takers** – They are willing to fail and to learn from their failures. Success is made up of individuals who are willing to take a risk even when others are pressing against the decision. They are resilient in the face of failure and always learn from their failures quickly.

8. **Time Masters** – They are mindful of their most precious asset—time. They actively guard their time and understand

how to maximize their productivity and focus on income-producing activities. They are energetic and capable of multi-tasking but innately have an ability to focus on each individual task at hand.

As you review the list above and determine you love the idea of being an innovator but don't have enough of the natural entrepreneurial traits to successfully launch a business, perhaps your ideal path would be as an *intrapreneur*.

An intrapreneur is an employee who has the creative traits of an entrepreneur but is not capable or interested in starting his or her own venture. They enjoy the corporate structure but desire the autonomy of creating that an entrepreneur is afforded. They want to be the fuel behind real change in a larger organization but don't necessarily want the risk involved.

If you have the burning desire to create and be a pivotal force to change but you really don't think you have the muscle to succeed as an entrepreneur, consider opportunities within the corporate structure that will allow you to leverage the existing corporate infrastructure and engage your entrepreneurial spirit.

LinkedIn and Google are two companies that have created a culture of intrapreneurship that aids them in maintaining their competitive edge. They encourage innovation and understand the entrepreneurial mind would be a terrible thing to waste! These opportunities exist, so go find one if that fits your need.

Let's assume you have assessed your core values and reviewed the traits above and your vision, hands down, is as an entrepreneur. Whether that definition is as a solopreneur or an individual who wants to rocket your business to a true entrepreneurial definition. What is the reality of starting your business? How do you make the transition?

The Scary Business of Transitioning into Your Own Business

Well, there is a cost to every choice we make. I don't believe in laying a bed of roses here. It is true. Every choice we make comes with a price.

The first step to a successful transition is to clearly understand the price you will pay. You will pay for the choice to entrepreneurship with risk. You will pay with loss of income as you build your business. You will pay with time as you intently focus on your new venture. There will be impact on your finances, your relationships and, from time-to-time, your sanity.

So please do not view the world of entrepreneurship with rose-colored lenses. Clear up the vision and work only in reality. No head in the sand tricks!

I have witnessed as a CPA and consultant far too many people who either buy a business or start a business without having a clear understanding of their financial position; they ultimately fail because they were not prepared. If you need help assessing your current situation and your future needs, hire a CPA, financial planner or business consultant who comes with glowing recommendations. Be very sure of the capital requirement necessary to bridge the gap between the start of your business and the time that you will actually be netting income from your new business.

Understand the start-up costs, any debt service and operating cost—and don't forget to estimate the big whopping chunk you will need to deliver to the taxing authorities. Project how much you will be able to derive from your business and understand what your personal financial requirements will be during your start-up phase.

Another bit of advice…Whatever you project as the time it will take you to get your business to a profitable level to provide you with enough income to cover all of your business and personal expenses—double it!

Most financial experts will advise you to have six-to-twelve months of savings. This depends on the business you are entering and the risk involved. You could in fact need three years' worth of back-up money (or three months), so be careful to project as carefully as possible.

It is sad when someone has started a business and they are just about at the pinnacle and run out of cash and the business fails. Do not underestimate this possibility, and please go into your new venture with eyes wide open.

Many people will decide to start their business while employed and slowly build the business until they are financially secure to transition to the new business full-time. Very smart idea.

A common question I receive is: When do I know it is time to make the leap?

I was in Bali working with Jack Canfield, the originator of the *Chicken Soup for the Soul®* series and co-author of *The Success Principles*, and he answered that question by saying, "It's like being a trapeze artist; you don't leap unless you are darn sure the other trapeze is swinging close enough that you can actually grab on."

I thought that was a perfect analogy. Don't leap unless you are sure the new business will sustain you.

Understand the impact of the investment of time as well. When you are starting a business, you will be strapped for time and all the people in your life will be affected too. You will need unending support from those around you as you enter the world of entrepreneurship and focus your energy away from others.

Communicating your need to focus and carving out time to balance your personal life with your new business will be very important.

Be aware of this time commitment and create a plan that will allow you to build the business in the time frame that will be comfortable for you and for those people who are closest to you.

Being realistic with the timing, and managing expectations effectively, will ease the tension as you bridge the financial gap. Remember that the goal is to transition smoothly and with as little friction as possible—it can and should be an enjoyable journey.

Creating a Vision for Your Business

After you have assessed your core values, identified what truly motivates you and have determined what level of entrepreneurship you would like to achieve, now you must create a clear vision for your business.

This step toward creating a successful business needs to be done vigorously, as this vision will inspire the framework for the blueprint of strategies and tactics that will pull the future vision into reality today.

Begin by asking yourself the following questions:

- Why will your business exist?
- Where do you see your business in one, three, five and 10 years?
- What specifically will you achieve at the interim periods?
- Last, but not least. What is your exit strategy? Are you creating this business to eventually sell? Do you intend to take the business public with an initial public offering (IPO)? Do you want your business to be an inherited asset? It is important to understand what your end game is.

Articulate your vision in writing and in great detail. When we commit our vision to paper it creates a dissonance in our mind between what we want and what is the reality today.

As we focus on our vision and our desires, that tension between vision and reality begins to set in motion the necessary action to merge that gap.

This is why having a powerful vision is so important. If you are not clear with what it is you want, it is going to be very hard to get there. It is like swimming without a buoy; you will aimlessly float with the current's force, zigzagging your way to some distant finish line. It will be a struggle, and in the end you may not achieve what it is you truly desire.

Now distill the vision for your business into a vision statement. We will use this in the next chapter as a basis to create your business plan.

An example of a vision statement is:

In five years, YourBiz.com will be the top technology resource for businesses by providing innovative ideas and solutions to businesses on a global basis.

From this vision statement a blueprint of strategies and tactics will be created to ensure achievement of this vision.

The VICTORY Take-Away

Entering the world of entrepreneurship and building a successful business requires that you have a clear vision of what you desire. Understanding your core values, the integration of your personal vision with the vision of your business, and assessing whether you have the "goods" and the traits that successful entrepreneurs possess will guide you to decide what level of entrepreneurship is right for you. Whether you become a solopreneur, entrepreneur or decide that intrapreneurship is right for you prior to entering the world of entrepreneurship, understanding the financial and time investment will pave the way to a smooth and successful transition to owning your own business.

You are now ready to take the next steps to create the blueprint to your VICTORY.

In chapter two, we will provide you with the tools to identify the gap between your future vision and the reality today and begin the planning phase of creating a profitable business.

Take Action

- Identify your core values utilizing Appendix A.
- Create a crystal clear vision for your business and personal life.
- Assess your personal traits and identify the level of entrepreneurship that is right for you.
- Understand your financial and timing requirements as you transition into entrepreneurship.

Chapter 2. Identify the Gap in the Game and Start Planning

THE GAP. THERE WILL ALWAYS BE a gap to close in business, or when racing in a triathlon.

In the bike portion of a tri the gap can be the hardest to close unless, like me, you like to climb hills. Being a bit compact in stature, being adept with the use of my gears and having a strategy gives me an advantage in picking off the competition on a hill!

But, when you crest the top and settle into the flats there is always the danger of becoming complacent. Lacking attention can cause the ground that was gained on the ascent to quickly be demolished by the competition and changing environment.

Let me explain. When you get to the flats, the steady geography can be the impetus to get too comfortable. Lack of concentration results in a loss in cadence, and before you know it, another gap opens and you have fallen behind.

Recognizing the gaps caused by a changing environment and creating a strategy to close the gap is critical to winning.

Competition is always fierce, and the external forces—whether from competition, economic distress or the changing landscape due to innovation—is an incessant threat to take an athlete or a business off course.

The questions are: Who will survive the pressure of the environment? Who will stand out in the crowd posing as the obvious choice for success?

The answer simply is: The competitors who pay attention to the gaps that form and take action.

Whether you are racing in a tri or competing in business, it's all the same—crowded and dynamic.

There is one guarantee, beyond taxes, in the lifecycle of a business, and that is the forever-changing business environment.

We have very little control over external forces, such as increased competition, political disruptions, changes in laws and advancement of technology, but we can control whether we choose to be proactive to our changing environment, or complacent and reactive.

I have witnessed many businesses that chose to "bury their head in the sand" and were not proactive in identifying the forces of change; their denial ensured that the business failed.

The key to developing a successful business is the ability to identify external forces that create gaps and incite opportunity.

The bottom line is that disruption creates opportunity. When businesses positively respond to a changing environment by identifying gaps in the market and responding by innovating, redefining their value proposition and creating more value to their customers than the competition, the business is elevated to new levels and profits rise.

At this point in your journey towards VICTORY you have established your personal vision in accordance with your core values, identified your true motivators, have committed to the level of entrepreneurship you desire and are confident in the vision for your business.

In this chapter, we will understand the importance of having a unique value proposition that fills the gap in your market so that your customers will think of your business as the only solution to their needs.

I will introduce the business model canvas, a tool to assess the viability of your business model. We'll talk about creating a business plan and the importance of recognizing this plan as a living document that should be repeatedly reviewed and changed.

And, in case you need funding to launch or grow your business, we'll talk about all the creative resources available beyond the traditional financial system.

In addition, you will read a contribution from an expert and learn how to present your business in such a compelling fashion that nobody will turn you away—not your prospects, or the banks!

What Is Your Value?

Now let's assess: Is the vision you have for your business viable, and is it filling a gap?

Your value proposition (VP) is a unique offer to solve a problem or fill an unmet need in the market that is not already being filled by the competition.

The VP is the foundation for a blueprint to create a successful business. Whether you are building a business or have been in business for many years, your value proposition is the reason people choose your product or service as their resource.

Value propositions change as businesses grow, markets change and customers' needs change. It is important to clearly identify and continuously reassess your business's value proposition in relation to the market.

So whether you are launching a spanking new business or are well established, evaluate your VP by asking the following questions:

- What value do you provide in the marketplace that is unique to your business?
- What will inspire your customers to choose you over the competition?
- How will you stand out against your competition?
- Will your business survive as external forces change your market?

Identifying and articulating a compelling value proposition is critical to building a successful business because if you don't have one, you are just one in a million businesses competing for the same customers, and it will be very difficult to get noticed.

A clearly articulated value proposition becomes the cornerstone of all marketing efforts and the driver of your profits.

How Do You Define Your Business's Value Proposition?

The first step toward formulating your value proposition is to define the unmet need for which your business will provide the solution.

The unmet need is the problem. Understanding the problem that your business will provide the solution to is key, and it will also enlighten you as to the urgency and degree of need.

Identify your target audience and their problem.

A few questions to consider:

1. Is the problem unavoidable? For example, is there a new government regulation going into effect that requires an organization to respond, creating an unavoidable need and most likely an urgent requirement?
2. Is the solution to the problem underserved? In other words, there's limited competition and resources have already been allocated to address the problem. Is there a conspicuous lack of organizations offering a solution to a particular need?
3. Is there no other solution to the problem available? In other words, a specific process is broken and the consequences are great. For example, someone gets fired if the problem isn't fixed?

If the answer to these three questions is positive, bingo—you have identified a void in the market.

The second step to developing your value proposition is to evaluate your offer.

Is it truly unique and consequently in demand? Having lower prices or the "best" customer service is not compelling or unique. These are expected attributes of any business.

Your offer must be a truly unique service or product that is easily adopted by customers, has only benefits and poses no, or very limited, risk to the customer. It must be disruptive to what your target audience is currently doing and provide a bridge to the gap in their unmet needs.

Understand the competition and evaluate your offer in relation to the competition. Understand who, what, where, when and how the competition is servicing the market. Make a list of the competition and really drill down into what exactly they are or are not providing to your target. Pay attention to their marketing messages. This will be useful later when it is time to create a marketing message that will differentiate your business.

Gather competitive intelligence by trolling the Internet and tracking competitors' activity. Watch them in their social media outreaches. Research your competitors and get to know what they offer, how they do it, how they define their target market and how they reach them.

Provide a unique service or product or alternative to what is currently offered. Is your solution innovative or disruptive…profoundly better than the alternative to what is being offered by your competition? Does your solution provide more gain for the customer than the trouble it will take to adopt your solution?

Talk to your target customers and uncover the challenges they are experiencing and are searching for a solution to. If you are already in business and looking to reposition yourself in your market, speak with your existing customers and ask them for feedback on your product or service.

Existing customers and prospects are great resources to gauge what is missing in your industry. I also recommend sending out a survey to existing customers. An anonymous survey typically will garner an honest evaluation of your existing business. (I recommend using SurveyMonkey.com.)

Too often, businesses fail because the owners were very passionate about their offer but didn't do enough research to establish if there was a need. Then they made the grave mistake of not assessing if their product or service is in fact different and filling a gap in the market.

A successful business will require passion, but the need must be identified and the offer evaluated. Doing these steps before you launch full board will save you time, money and potentially failure. So before your take Aunt Edna's fruitcake global be sure you have a strong value proposition!

Now that you have identified the gap in the market and created a strong value proposition as to what differentiates your product or service from what is currently available, it is time to review your business model.

The Business Model

Reviewing your intended business model will help you move towards preparing a business plan. Your business model identifies how your business will make money—for example, franchise, direct sales, subscription, distribution, etc. Think of your model as being the architecture of your business.

Your business plan will detail the specific goals of the business and the strategies and tactics for each function that will support your business model.

I recommend the Business Model Canvas as a tool to guide you to assess your business. You can find it at www.businessmodelgeneration.com.

The Business Model Canvas is brilliant and was developed by Alexander Osterwalder. I often use this methodology when working with clients in assessing a new business or an introduction of a new segment within an existing business.

The success of your business plan is dependent upon the premise that your business model is solid and will be profitable.

In summary, the Business Model Canvas drills down the vision of your business by addressing nine key elements:

1. **Value Proposition**. The unique offer that your business presents over your competition.
2. **Customer Segments**. Simply, who your customer is and what challenge your business is solving.
3. **Channels**. How will the product or service will be distributed?

4. **Customer Relationships**. How will product buzz be created, interest incited and demand established?

5. **Cost Structure**. What are the costs, both fixed and variable, of running your business?

6. **Key Activities**. What must your organization do to succeed?

7. **Key Resources**. Who are your suppliers?

8. **Key Partners**. Who are the supporting entities that are essential to the success of your business?

9. **Revenue Streams**. What are the revenue sources?

Once you have created your business canvas, test the model by gathering as much feedback as possible from all stakeholders. Analyze the feedback and revise your model as needed.

This is the time to pivot your model based on feedback. In the business model assessment phase, remember, it's all just paper! There is no real financial loss, so review and revise as much as needed to gain assurance and confidence that your model is poised for success.

Once you have received validation that your model will perform, now it is time to create all of the nitty-gritty details as to how to execute.

The Business Plan

How can you run a race if you don't have a map of the course? There is no winning if you are unsure of the direction you are going and don't have a strategy to get there. Your business plan is your map to move your business towards realizing your vision.

More often than I would like, a client will ask me to write their business plan for them. No, no and no is my answer!

Yes, I understand that you need help understanding your numbers, identifying your targets, etc. I know, I understand the fear associated with developing your own plan; however, you must write your own plan.

It is imperative that you understand your business intimately and creating your own business plan will allow you to see the strengths and weaknesses of each intricate detail in your business. Writing your business plan will force you to review every aspect of your business with a critical eye.

Do not underestimate the importance of this step in launching your business. This process will steer you to make critical decisions.

A business plan is a living document that serves as a guide to achieve your vision.

Successful businesses that have been in operation for years continuously review their business plans and revise as necessary to adjust for changes in the market. Once a business launches and is on a trajectory of growth, the plan should change to reflect the growth.

The biggest mistake a business can make is to slip into complacency and never review or revise their business plan. There is a tendency to think a plan is only used for the purpose of attracting investors or bank financing, but it is a document that should be continuously utilized as a map to ensure continued success.

So with a strategic mindset, begin developing your business plan utilizing the following outline:

Step 1 – Perform market research to gain an understanding of your industry, competitors and customers.

1. Research your market and analyze current trends in the industry. If your business is a new venture, this will guide you to uncover what opportunities exist that will be profitable. If it is an existing business, market research can bring to light unfulfilled customer needs.

   There are two types of market research: primary and secondary, and both should be investigated.

   Primary research consists of gathering information through surveys, interviewing existing or potential customers, or utilizing focus groups that can give you direct feedback. Ask your targets what challenges they are experiencing, how they make their purchasing decisions and where they see room for improvement within the current market. Ask them about price, delivery and customer service.

   Secondary research is data that has already been published. This research can help you segment your market, and identify and analyze competitors. Easily accessible online, a few great sources for secondary market research are trade associations and publications in your industry. The U.S. Economic

Census and (if you are a business-to-business model) Dun & Bradstreet are also great resources.

2. Detail who your competitors are and why your prospective customers currently buy from them. What are their advantages and disadvantages?
3. Articulate your value proposition. What differentiates you from the competition? Why will your customers be inspired to choose your product or service? Which competitors will you displace?
4. Identify and describe specifically who your customers are. How will you reach them?
5. Describe in detail your product or service offering and how much it will cost to produce or deliver.
6. Identify what resources will be required to launch your business: financial, skills, talent, production, etc.

Step 2 – Detail Your Plan.

1. Identify the business infrastructure—processes and systems—that will be required to support your business.
2. Create pro forma financials (*pro forma financials* are statements based on anticipated results) on a monthly, quarterly and annual basis. Project conservatively as well as optimistically, while being realistic in sales revenue, margins, expenses and projected profits. Create a budget and forecast for a minimum of two years.
3. Identify and create a two-year marketing plan.
4. Create a two-year sales plan.

5. Identify your exit strategy. Do you intend to sell after a period of time? Would you like to take your company public with an IPO? Would you like your family to inherit the business?

6. If you are going after capital investment, pretend you are the investor/banker and answer their questions.

Note: In chapter three, we will discuss in depth the seven pillars of a business: operations, marketing, sales, customer relations, finance, human resources and technology. I will present various strategies and tactics that will be utilized in the planning phase of your business plan.

Step 3 – Write your plan.

I was having dinner with a friend of mine who is a banker and we were chatting about new businesses seeking financing. I asked him about the quality of business plans he has received and he said that the best plan he ever received came from a snowboard company and was hand-written on an 11 x 14 sheet of paper.

Moral of the story: your plan does not have to be a fancy document!

It does, however, need to offer a complete picture, be realistic and support all projections. There are many online products that can help you with the process of writing a plan— however, I always think they sound canned. I encourage you to be creative and develop your own plan from scratch.

The following are the key components of a business plan:

1. **Executive Summary**. This section is the most important segment of the plan as it tends to be read thoroughly by the person reviewing the plan, while the rest of the plan may be afforded just a cursory glance in search of specific answers.

   It needs to answer the who, what, when, how and why of your product or service offering. Who are the key stakeholders? What is the objective and vision of the organization? Why does your business need to exist, when and how will you launch?

   The executive summary also will include a summary of production, marketing and sales. Also included is a financial overview indicating capital needs and financial projections.

   The executive summary should be very succinct. If this is being utilized to gain capital investment, put yourself in the reader's shoes and be sure you are answering the questions you would have if you were investing in the business.

2. **Market Analyses**. This information will be sourced from the investigation you performed in reaching your value proposition. This section will thoroughly describe the industry, projection of trends, and your position within the market segment.

3. **Company Description**. This section describes in detail your business: the vision, mission, organizational

structure and key people within the organization. In addition, the company description should include a detailed description and development plan of the product or service offered.

4. **Marketing Plan**. Explain to your reader how you will attract customers. What methods will you employ to raise awareness of your product or service? Divulge your brand position and how that will drive your marketing efforts.

5. **Sales Plan.** Present your specific sales strategies and tactics in this section. Your strategies are the plans that support your sales goals. The tactics are the specific steps that will be taken to carry out the strategy. Will you drive sales online? Will your business reside in a brick and mortar building? What is your sales outreach strategy? Where is your sales market? What is your projection for growth and how will you manage growth?

6. **SWOT Analysis**. This is a method to identify, evaluate and present the **S**trengths, **W**eaknesses, **O**pportunities and potential **T**hreats in your business. This technique was created by Albert Humphrey in the 1960s and introduced at a Stanford Research Institute conference. This process aids in evaluating the impact of internal and external forces on an organization's ability to achieve the intended mission.

Strengths are the characteristics of the product, service or organizational structure that provide a competitive advantage.

Weaknesses are those disadvantages that you are seeking to overcome that leave you vulnerable to competition. Note that any weakness presented needs a projected solution.

Opportunities are those aspects of the plan that can be exploited to create success in the organization and bring future growth.

Threats are those possibilities that could challenge the business. For example, an unknown competitor emerges. Each threat should also present a projected positive response to the threat.

A SWOT analysis lets your reader know that you have thoroughly explored your business and are aware of the internal and external forces that can impact your business and that you have strategized accordingly.

7. **Capital Requirements.** If the purpose of your plan is to seek funding, this is the section that quantifies the need and the projected timing of the need. Also, it relays the purpose for the financial need, or how the funds will be utilized (working capital, research and development, etc.). In addition, your investors will

want to have a clear projection of their return on investment, and timing.

If there is not a capital investment need, this section should include two years of pro forma financials and include in the financial notes all of the assumptions used as a basis for the projections.

8. **Summary.** This should be a very short, clear and concise summary of the overall plan. Think of this summary as a vision statement that captures the business's purpose and the results that will be created.

After you have created your business plan, ask yourself "Does this make sense?" This is a very simple question. You have investigated, analyzed, scrutinized and hopefully turned your plan inside and out. So does it make sense?

If the answer is yes, go forward and let's begin to create the strategies and tactics that will support your plan.

If the answer is no, do not pass go. Save yourself and your potential investors time and money and rework your plan or abandon ship altogether.

As I mentioned earlier, I am not a fan of having someone else create your business plan for you. That being said, there is value to reaching out for counsel once your plan has been developed. A CPA, a friend who is a marketing guru, or an attorney can be of great assistance in reviewing the plan.

Before you present your plan to an investor or begin creating the strategies and tactics to support the plan, getting an outside person to poke holes is an exercise worth submitting to.

An unbiased opinion can highlight weaknesses that you as the owner of the plan cannot see.

Funding

Now that you have a solid business plan perhaps you have identified a gap in funding. There are many options available today, such as traditional banks, the Small Business Association, angel investors and venture capitalists. Let's not forget we have crowdfunding too!

Before I go into great detail on the various options for funding a start-up, it is important that you understand that with every funding option you will give up something. Whether the expense of interest on a loan or giving an equity position, there is a price to be paid for diversifying your risk. The more risk you give up, the less reward you receive.

You also may be required to give up control or, at the very least, you will have increased reporting to your stakeholders. This increased reporting, or possibly rights to decision-making, can become distracting and can slow down your progress greatly.

These are just a few considerations as you assess your capital requirements and sources.

Here is a review of several funding options:

Bootstrapping. I am a big fan of leveraging your personal assets, as this option keeps 100% of the reward for your efforts with you. However, this means you are taking 100% of the risk.

When considering funding your venture, it is important that you not only consider the funding necessary for your new business but also the funding that will be necessary to bridge the period of time between the launch of your business and the time you as an owner can draw funds from profits.

Friends and Family. My position on this is "no." Dear Lord, Thanksgiving can be hard enough without answering return on investment questions or having Aunt Betty offering her opinion on the latest news in your industry. That being said, if you are from a kickass wealthy family who loves you so much you can do no wrong, go for it!

Crowdfunding. Sometimes it takes a crowd, and this system of collaboration on the web with the purpose of funding a specific project is great. Typically, they have focused on creative projects. Spike Lee utilized crowdfunding to gather up money for one of his movies.

Kickstarter is one of the most popular crowdfunding sites. The basics are that people pre-buy your product but no equity or debt is exchanged. Be aware, however, that regulations on this financial vehicle may change with the implementation of the JOBS Act, which is paving the way for investment crowdfunding.

Venture Capital (VC). This is the crew that represents institutional investors who are looking for the latest and greatest next hot investment and a corresponding high return to match. These people are pros and if they think your idea is hot and that you are on the precipice of massive growth, then get your team together and be sure the VC is a good choice for you.

Angel Investors. Everyone loves an angel. These groups are made up of wealthy people who are interested in funding startups. These investors provide capital in exchange for debt or an equity position. Angels can be sophisticated and provide advice—not a bad deal.

Pitching Your Product or Service

So now you have created your business plan and identified a need for funding perhaps. Now how do you pitch your idea? How do you make your presentation so compelling that you will get a YES?

We deliver our message every day to new prospects, existing customers, employees and a myriad of stakeholders. A perfect pitch will ensure not only that you will attract investors, if needed, but you will drive your sales every time you present to a prospect or customer.

So how do you tell a story that immediately incites interest from your audience and addresses their concerns and challenges in a way that makes your value proposition and business memorable?

To answer this very important question on how to deliver your message in a compelling manner that gives the results desired, I have brought in **Chris Westfall**.

Chris is the author of *The NEW Elevator Pitch* and the co-creator of The 118 Pitch Course with Jeffrey Hayzlett. On the web at westfallonline.com and on Twitter at @westfallonline.

Contribution from the
National Elevator Pitch Champion Chris Westfall

In business, the stories you tell will teach people how to treat you, how to invest in your business and how to follow your ideas.

As a business leader, if you want to influence and persuade with your message, you've got to understand how to create a story that's compelling. The key to delivering a great message isn't in the sound of your vowels or your gestures or even the words that you choose. A great delivery starts at a place that's quite unexpected.

As an entrepreneur, you're intimately involved in every aspect of your business. Maybe some of the advice in this book has helped you to delegate or step back from non-essential tasks, but there is an undeniable link between you and your business. Wouldn't you agree?

So, when someone says, "Tell me a little bit more about your business. What is it exactly that you do?" it's easy to imagine that this is a simple invitation to begin talking about yourself.

But great delivery isn't that simple.

It's actually simpler.

In life, it's no secret that you get what you expect. Where you put your attention is where you will find your results.

By putting your attention on the ideas in this book, you will find new results and new strategies for your business.

The same concept applies to great delivery. The secret to great delivery is as simple as your focus.

When someone says, "Tell me a little bit about yourself," it's easy to imagine that statement as an open door to talk about who you are and what you do.

But don't fall into that trap.

Because "Tell me a little bit about yourself" is actually a trick question.

Think about it for a second. What's really being asked is, "Tell me a little bit about yourself…and what you might be able to do for ME."

It's only human nature. People are focused on their own interests. Just as you read these words, you are filtering the ideas of this book through your own experience.

The constant question is not "What does this information mean?"

The question is "What does this information mean to me?"

So, if you want your delivery to matter—and, by the way, if you want your story to be heard, your delivery always matters—you've got to create the right focus. You've got to demonstrate an understanding of human nature and put your attention where it matters most.

On your listener.

In other words, you've got to turn the mirror around. When it comes time to talk about yourself and your business, you've got to shift your focus.

Why?

Because the best message—whether you tweet it or tell it—starts with your listener. Your website, your branding, your story has to create some sort of connection with your audience. Otherwise, your delivery is lost.

If your story doesn't involve your listener, how can you expect your listener to get involved?

If you're an analytical person like me, you may share a common belief; the belief that "the numbers speak for themselves." I often address this mindset when working with coaching clients in health sciences, technology and finance.

Unfortunately, the numbers never speak for themselves. Neither do the drawings or the three-year projections or the regression analysis you just completed.

Similarly, your Facebook page, LinkedIn profile and company website are also incomplete. What's missing from the story? In a word, YOU.

If you want your delivery to matter, you've got to focus on what matters most.

Don't start your story by talking in the first person (that's I – me – my). (Remember the famous words from the classic tale of the white whale by Herman Melville? "Call me Ishmael" is the opener for Moby Dick—the great example of first-person narrative). Do you often find yourself speaking in the first person? How many "I's" do you have?

It's easy to get caught up in the idea of a first-person narrative when it comes time to tell your story. As an entrepreneur, you will want to focus on what the business means to you, what you've built within the company and where you'd like to go with your vision.

But that's actually the wrong focus if you want your delivery to matter. Don't focus on a first-person narrative. You've got to make the second person first.

Second person is "You." Not you, the person reading this book, but "you"— your audience.

I was meeting a coaching client, a medical sales professional, for the first time. "Chris," she said to me, "I've heard so much about you. Why don't you tell me a little bit about yourself?"

Aha! That's an easy one, I thought to myself.

"Well, I'm the national elevator pitch champion."

"Wow! That's great!" she said, enthusiastically. And then, "What's an elevator pitch?"

By blurting and focusing on my story, I had failed to connect with the most important person in the room. I had failed to create a story that engaged my listener.

In other words, my delivery was far from excellent. In fact, it was cryptic and confusing.

Have you ever had a similar experience? You know, where you start talking about the thoughts and ideas that are racing through your head, without taking the time to take in your audience, your listener? The result is usually a blank stare or "Huh?" or a return to texting—without so much as a second thought.

You see, there are too many messages. Too many distractions. That's why your delivery is more important than ever.

If you don't consider your delivery—and your audience—your story is just lost in the noise. And, if your story feels like you're reading your LinkedIn profile to someone or quoting chapter and verse from your latest product specs...Well, is it any wonder that people are bored, customers are disappearing and employees aren't listening?

It's a fact of life that we are all focused on ourselves. But excellent delivery goes beyond your personal list of features and benefits, and considers what your story means to your listener.

If you're proposing a change for your employees, your board or your partners, how does this move affect each of those unique audiences? How does your conversation take a 360-degree approach to the situation (instead of a purely self-centered approach)?

By making the second person first, you can take your message and your delivery to a whole new level. And, when you change your focus, you can change your results.

Focusing on your listener means using more "you" in the story. In other words, phrasing your branding and your narrative not just on the details but also on what the details mean to your audience.

So, as you consider taking your delivery to the next level, stop focusing on your story.

Your story is solid. After all, there's no one in the world who knows you and your business better than you do. But what about the connection you need to make your message matter?

The details and the numbers are important, there's no doubt. So are your experience and your objectives. But if you want to demonstrate real business insight—and create a powerful personal connection in your delivery— make sure you place your attention on what really matters most: your listener.

Thank you, Chris!

I was fortunate to have met Chris through a mastermind group, and his insights as to how to make a pitch compelling are invaluable.

It doesn't matter what your product or service is. We are all pitching all day, every day—whether it is to a prospect, an existing customer or our children. We are conversing in a manner meant to persuade our audience, and if you take Chris's advice you will be much more effective and have tremendous impact on the profitability of your business. You may even be able to get your kids in bed on time!

When I first met Chris and he asked me what I did, I also made the mistake of not focusing on my listener, and I didn't give a thought as to how to relay my message in a manner that would connect with him or his needs.

Needless to say I think Chris' head tilted a bit in puzzlement as I spoke. He is a smart man, so he clearly understood what my business was about, but he had no clue how it related to his business or how I could positively impact him.

So after we had our discussion about a successful elevator pitch and he opened that door and again asked, "Chris, tell me about yourself," I responded by saying:

"Well, Chris, you know how as a small business owner we are inundated with information and don't really know what strategies will actually produce more sales in our business, and because our time is so limited it is so frustrating to try to figure it all out?" At this point, Chris didn't tilt his head but leaned in indicating to me I had his interest, so I continued…

"Well, I help small business owners save time and money by advising them as to what strategies to implement in their business that will create more profits. Basically, I take away the frustration and make success much easier for them. How would that make you feel to know that you have someone who is able to see the whole picture of your business and guide you to leverage your strengths and help you shore up the weaknesses creating more profit?"

So this is my personal elevator pitch. Since I have been enlightened by Chris Westfall, my conversations have gone deeper, they have been more productive and my conversion rates have gotten much higher.

I encourage you to read his book, *The NEW Elevator Pitch*, and check out his course The 118 Pitch Course on the web at westfallonline.com. (You can find Chris' book online at chrisvanderzyden.com/NewElevatorPitch.)

After all, you only have eight seconds to gain interest and one hundred and ten seconds to reel them in. Tick-tock.

The VICTORY Take-Away

The gap in the marketplace created by constant innovation is an opportunity to capitalize and create the successful business you have envisioned.

By harnessing the energy of disruption and identifying the unique value your product or service brings to your target customers, you can create a business model that will create an enormously profitable business. But, of course, planning is the key.

A strong business plan will pave the way to an easier launch and sustained success. The business-planning phase is an opportunity to work out the kinks in your business on paper, with the safety net of not losing any real money.

Don't waste the opportunity the planning phase offers by scurrying through this process. Create your plan with intensity and look for the weaknesses.

If your planning surfaces the need for capital investment, luckily there are more options available today than ever before. Once you have chosen the right funding channel, be sure your pitch is perfect to ensure you get the dough needed to launch successfully.

Recognize that a perfect pitch will also go a long way towards increasing your sales.

Take Action

- Identify the gaps in your market sector and evaluate your value proposition in relation to your competitors.
- Review your business model and analyze the viability of all supporting elements.
- Begin your business plan and prepare to create your strategy and tactics in all seven pillars of business in the next chapter.
- Exercise your elevator pitch and ask yourself, "Is it focused on your listener and creating real engagement?"

Race Day: Taking Action

SCAN TO VIEW RACE DAY VIDEO

chrisvanderzyden.com/action

Chapter 3. Creating the Strategies and Tactics to Win

HOW MUCH DO I GIVE OUT in the swim with two more events forthcoming? How many people will I plan to take out when climbing the hills, and how much energy do I need to reserve to ensure that I will succeed on the bike? If I overextend early in the race, will I die in the run? When will I eat during the race? How much and when is the best time to drink? These are the questions that need to be answered when creating a strategy to race.

I assure you, there is no winning without a strategy and supporting tactics. Most people would not think of competing in a race without first creating a strategy and a plan of action to train. Why would you launch a business without creating rock-solid strategies and tactics to follow as your map to success? You wouldn't, unless you weren't quite sure what to do.

In this chapter, you will learn about the various disciplines in a business and the importance of creating the strategies, tactics and action steps necessary to drive success.

Once you have created the vision for your business, identified your value proposition and developed a tested business model, now the strategies and tactics need to be created to support the business plan.

Developing a profitable business is not rocket science, I assure you. With careful planning and execution you can create as profitable a business as you choose.

There is no VICTORY without a strategy, supporting tactics and action. Running your business at the platinum level will require that you take the time to plan for your VICTORY.

One of the primary reasons for a high failure rate in small businesses is not enough time is spent creating a very specific, focused strategic plan with supporting tactics to achieve the desired result. Many times I have heard the excuses: There is not enough time, I don't have the expertise, I don't know what to do.

In this chapter, we will explore each of the main segments that create a successful business. From the information presented, you will identify the strategy and supporting tactics that will be part of your winning blueprint to building a successful business.

There are seven main pillars in a profitable business: operations, marketing, sales, customer service, finance, human resources and technology.

For those readers who already have an existing business and are searching to elevate your business, each pillar should be evaluated, weaknesses identified and a plan created to improve upon the weaknesses and leverage the strengths of your business.

PILLAR #1 – Operations

Operations refers to how the primary purpose of your business functions, including the physical necessities and resources required for your business to operate and produce and deliver your product or service to your customers.

Every business should have a documented operational plan to ensure efficiencies within the organization.

In developing the plan, consider how your business will operate, produce and distribute your product or service. Depending upon whether your model is manufacturing or in the service industry, your focus in operations will be different.

Answer the following questions to develop your operating plan:

- Where will the business operate?
- What hours will the business operate?
- What kind of premises, production facility or office space will be required to perform your business?
- What equipment will be necessary?
- Who will the suppliers be?
- How will the product be created?
- What production lead-time will be required?
- What channels will be utilized to distribute the product or service?
- What type of sales force will be needed?

- How will the customers be continuously serviced and nurtured?

I recommend documenting everything your business does in all areas and creating an operations manual to ensure operational efficiency.

After you have created an operational plan, continuously execute a systematic review by analyzing the operational results in comparison to the plan. A continuous review will alert you to the need for any revisions necessary in order to ensure your business runs smoothly.

PILLAR #2 – Marketing

The all-important driver of profits is marketing.

Marketing is about positioning your product and is best known in the marketing realm as the four Ps:

- **Product**: Delivering the right product or service to your target market. This speaks to having the right product to offer to your audience. Again, your product or service must have a unique selling point that separates it from the competition so that demand is created.

- **Price**: Selling your product or service at a price that is agreeable to your target audience. For a product, the price will be determined by the cost to produce and then compared to the competition. In a service business, the price is based on the result or value your customer receives. Remember that the price and value delivered must incentivize the customer to return again and again.

- **Promotion**: Creating a memorable message that is delivered consistently and cohesively through various marketing channels.

- **Place**: Distributing your product or service in a manner where it can be easily found. Identify where your targets are and through which channels your product or service needs to be distributed to reach your customer.

The four Ps are a very simplistic description of the marketing process, but it is necessary that each P be on target with your audience in order to be successful in the market.

In this section, we are going to focus on Promotion and Place in the marketing matrix, as the product and price will be variable to each reader.

Customers will not come knocking on your door if they don't know about you or your product or service—thus, the importance of developing a very clever marketing strategy. Hanging a shingle out announcing that you are open for business is not enough.

Here is a standard conversation I frequently have with a new client who is struggling:

> CLIENT: I don't have enough business and I'm not making enough money.
>
> ME: Well, what is your marketing program?
>
> CLIENT: I go to networking meetings.

ME: How often do you go to networking meetings?

CLIENT: Every now and then. Well, about four times a year.

ME: What do you do at the events?

CLIENT: I give out my business card.

ME: What else do you do to market?

CLIENT: I have a website.

ME: How are you driving traffic to the website?

CLIENT: The website is on my business card.

ME: What other ways do you market your business?

CLIENT: Huh?

You must market consistently, through a variety of channels and with a strategy behind your actions. Marketing is the muscle that communicates your product or service's value proposition to your target audience. It is the fuel for converting prospects to sales.

When marketing is done correctly and consistently, it will create a never-ending stream of fabulously loyal, profitable customers. This is a textbook definition of marketing.

For me, marketing is about having a complete understanding of your customer and creating an emotional attachment to your brand as the solution to their challenges. Understanding who your ideal customer is entails identifying the demographics of your prospect, such as age, gender, income level and education.

In addition to demographic information, which informs *who* will buy your product or service, understanding the psychographics of *why* a person buys is also important. Psychographics are the attitudes, beliefs, values and emotions that drive your prospect to buy.

By segmenting and understanding your ideal customer, a marketing message can be developed that will be tailored to your target audience and relayed in their language, creating an emotional attachment to your product or service.

So how do we attract loyal customers?

At the nucleus of the marketing strategy is the brand. Your brand, as Jeffrey Hayzlett loves to convey over and over, is merely the promise delivered. What experience are you delivering to your customer?

Developing a Memorable Brand

"When people use your BRAND as a VERB, that is Remarkable."

~ Meg Whitman

For your brand to be used as a verb, your brand must be memorable and:

- Deliver your promise clearly
- Relay your credibility
- Make an emotional connection with your target
- Motivate your audience to take action
- Create unsurpassed customer loyalty

I have brought **branding expert Joy Murphy** to contribute her insights as to how to develop a brand that will communicate that your business is the only solution to your target audience's problem. Here is what she has to say:

Contribution from Branding Expert Joy Murphy

What's in a Brand? A LOT!

A brand is far more than a logo, trademark or tagline. It is the CONNECTION you create with your audience and the way in which your business relates to the world.

Your brand is every experience, emotion and association a person has with your company, product or service. It is the promise of what you will deliver, the values you stand for, and the expectation your clients can have for doing business with you.

Great brands have clearly defined missions; personalities and points of differentiation that make them easy to recognize and understand.

Coca-Cola. Polo Ralph Lauren. TOMS Shoes. Starbucks. Tiffany & Co. Zappos.com. They reinforce ideals of consistency, quality, performance and value in the hearts and minds of their customers by delivering on their promises again and again—in every interaction and with every person they serve.

Great brands connect in a personal way, evoking emotion, inspiring loyalty and creating a premium value for that connection—for the brand.

Whether branding a company, product, service or individual, the principles for developing a dynamic, powerful and reliable brand are the same.

To follow are six key areas of development, including specific questions to consider and steps to take when defining, building and living your brand.

1. Define the Audience, Need and Competitive Environment

Begin by defining who your target audience is and the personal, societal or practical need that your business, product or service will fill.

Get endlessly curious. Do your research and find out all there is to know about both your constituents and your competitors. Spend the time and effort to understand what is already out there and what may still be missing.

Once you have a thorough understanding of the need, then you can position your unique business, product and personality to fill it.

- What are the offerings already out in the market?

- What are strengths and weaknesses of those products or services?

- What do your customers' want that is not being offered—or not being well executed?

Zappos.com was born out of a need for shoes. In 1999, Nick Swinmurn found himself searching the mall and limited online sites of the time, but there were no major retailers providing large inventories and assortments of shoes. Zappos.com was created to fill a need for accessibility to the best and widest selection of shoes—brands, styles, colors, sizes and widths—for anyone, in any city, any time.

2. Determine Your Unique Mission, Promise and Value Proposition

Brands are both functional and emotional. While your product or service will address a customer's practical needs, great brands create connection by building trust, aligning values and fulfilling on expectation.

Consider how you want your customers to think of your brand and the attributes that support that image. By maximizing on your unique credentials and strengths, you'll win a place in the market that your competitors can't touch.

- What is your brand mission or intention?

- What does your brand stand for—what are the values behind it and the feeling it wants to deliver?

- How do your specific qualifications, skills, experience and style create a unique opportunity and experience for your customer?

- What is the promise that you are willing to make to the world and deliver on every day in every way?

Zappos.com began to take off when CEO Tony Hseih (pronounced "Shay") evolved the brand promise from one of function—providing the best selection of shoes—to one that was infused with a value proposition like no other company in the space. Zappos.com would provide the absolute best customer service to its audience, delivering a WOW experience that they could not find anywhere else.

The company instantly became famous for offering its customers free shipping—both ways. But it also began to stand out for providing live, personal customer-service interaction 24 hours a day, for readily upgrading clients to VIP status (next-day delivery, still free), and engaging customers with enthusiasm, fun, personality, passion and respect.

Most importantly, Zappos.com won customer loyalty through their dedication and consistency, delivering on their promises with every client interaction, every day, and in every way.

3. Develop Your Brand Name, Personality and Marks

Your company name, logo, tagline, website, marketing materials and more are the methods by which your brand message and promise are conveyed to the world.

Infusing these elements with unique personality traits will give your brand energy and create greater connection with your customers. How a business looks, thinks, speaks and acts is as vital to its credibility and sustainability as the product or service itself. Choose your style and execute on it in every form.

- What are the personality traits you want your brand/business to convey? Is it daring and edgy?

Conservative and serious? Playful? Creative? Sophisticated? Simple?

- Choose a business name that conveys the image you want to evoke in people's minds. Ask your best customers what the name means to them— you'll gain additional loyalty by showing that their opinions are important.

- Develop a tagline that quickly and concisely gives customers insight into your market position. Does it align with the characteristics of your brand promise and personality? Is it easy to remember and understand?

- Create a logo in the colors and style appropriate to your brand and message. Is it bright and fun? Dark and mysterious? Bold? Fresh? Clean? Complex?

Zappos.com's (derived from *zapatos*, the Spanish word for shoes) clearly defined personality is fun, adventurous, creative, quirky and driven by an unwavering commitment to service.

Not only do these traits come across in the company's logo treatment (simple, yet non-traditional lettering punctuated with an exclamation point in the shape of a footprint) and tagline ("Powered by service"), but they are so integral to the Zappos.com DNA that the company has included these traits in its 10 Core Values that influence everything it does.

Remember the much celebrated and highly entertaining Zappos.com TV ads that featured real recordings of customer service calls being acted out by puppets? A quirky, fun and well-differentiated creative idea that also demonstrated the company's promise of live customer relations operators engaging shoppers in a uniquely personal, WOW service experience.

Zappos' Core Values

1. Deliver WOW through service
2. Embrace and drive change
3. Create fun and a little weirdness
4. Be adventurous, creative and open-minded
5. Pursue growth and learning
6. Build open and honest relationships with communication
7. Build a positive team and family spirit
8. Do more with less
9. Be positive and determined
10. Be humble

4. Launch Your Brand!

You're ready to launch your brand and tell your story in a big way. Leverage the relationships, media and technologies that are aligned with your brand essence and values to help spread the word about your business and its unique place in the market.

- Share your news! Use your network, resources and creativity to spread the word and get people talking. Choose social media outlets that are appropriate for your brand--i.e. build a Facebook page, start a Twitter account and create a LinkedIn profile that support your mission and reinforce your promise.

- Create a thought leadership platform. Writing a blog is one of the best ways to establish expertise, create connection, build loyalty and raise visibility with potential customers. Have a clearly defined point of view that aligns with your brand personality, and provide valuable content to your readers, giving them a reason to "like," "share" and come back for more.

- Build an army of Brand Ambassadors. Establish relationships with key influencers in your business space and get them talking about your brand in a positive light. Help to build awareness for each other's brands by referring customers, sharing content and inviting them to contribute guest posts to your blog site.

Zappos.com CEO Tony Hseih may not have launched the original company, but he implemented every tool that was available and appropriate to help the brand explode.

Understanding that the customer can be your most loyal and influential brand ambassador, he took to Twitter as a way of engaging consumers and deepening the personal connection. From impromptu party invitations (posted *only* on Twitter, making the events exclusive to followers) to photos and video of the company's "Bald and Blue

Day" when all employees shave their heads or dye their hair blue (there's that quirky, fun and "a little weird" company personality again) to musings, pop culture, favorite quotes, and Zappos in the news.

He also began creating a distinct thought leadership platform, authoring ***Delivering Happiness: A Path to Profits, Passion and Purpose***, and sharing his business formula for spreading happiness—or "Zappiness"—at premier leadership events, such as South by Southwest (SXSW), Women's Wear Daily (WWD) CEO Summits, and numerous digital retail and entrepreneurial conferences.

5. Live Your Brand!

Make the commitment to live your brand promise in every way. Set an intention to reinforce your value proposition each and every time you interact with someone—whether a customer, employee, vendor, partner or competitor. Consider what impression you want them to have of your business, and become the primary reflection of your brand.

- How do your personal and professional lives align or conflict with your brand values?

- How does your company culture reflect the values of the brand?

- What do your customers, employees and partners say about their experiences with your brand?

- If your best customers spent a day working inside of your company, what would they see and experience that would surprise them, delight them, comfort them or disappoint them?

From the CEO down—through the creative team, customer service reps, facilities managers and on—the Zappos "family," as they refer to themselves, live their brand in every way. Just visit the About section of Zappos.com to view one of many videos that shows how they embrace and execute the 10 Core Values (# 3, Create Fun and a Little Weirdness, is particularly well represented!).

Further, because the company's #1 Core Value, Delivering WOW Through Service is also the brand promise to its customers, every Zappos.com employee at every level of the company participates in a four-week customer loyalty training program.

6. Use Your Brand Promise to Inspire Evolution, Drive Decisions and Create the Future

Even the best brands run the risk of becoming old and stale if they are not continuously infused with fresh ideas and creativity. Your brand promise, values and personality are the benchmarks by which you'll test decisions for how your company will evolve and grow.

- How do potential new product lines align with your brand promise and values?

- How do your audiences want to engage with your brand and receive information?

- How can your brand authentically evolve to satisfy the changing needs of your customers?

- Revisit your vision for the company. Where will the brand be in three, five, ten years?

Zappos believes that one day (probably sooner than we think), 30% of all retail transactions will be made online and that people will choose to buy from the company that provides the best of service and selection.

Their intention is to be that company. And their brand promise is the benchmark by which they build their culture and make business decisions that will get them there.

They recognized early on that competing on price was not the game they wanted to play, so discounting never became part of their brand promise—and never will.

Instead, the company understood that as long as they were able to deliver on their commitment of providing the absolute best service, they could expand into almost any product category they chose.

Today Zappos.com sells shoes, apparel, handbags, home décor, beauty and more, successfully, because they are able to execute on those categories while delivering great service and a WOW customer experience.

Any category that might jeopardize that promise is not aligned with their brand and does not become part of the company.

Whatever type of business you are building, brand development is your opportunity to get creative, take some risks and have fun along the way! Never stop adding to your own expertise or finding new ways to connect with your audience. And always, always stay true to your brand.

The brand is the core of a marketing plan.

With your brand in mind, now develop a marketing strategy with this four-step process:

1. **Review your value proposition, your target audience and your SWOT analysis**. Based on your VP and your SWOT, clearly state your marketing objectives. What do you expect to accomplish through your marketing plan (i.e. "We will sell 50,000 units at a 22% margin within the first quarter.")?

2. **Segment your target market**. For example, if your target is a woman, further segment the group by age. This is about narrowing the field to further define what sector of your audience the marketing message will be sent to. The narrower the target, the easier it is to create an impactful message.

3. **Organize a marketing strategy** utilizing the channels that resonate with your market segment. Identify what type of marketing collateral will be utilized, and through which channels, to reach your target customers. Below, I discuss the various channels available to relay your message. Each option has its own positives and negatives. Your choice of channel will depend on where your target market receives

information and, in large part, how much of a budget is available for marketing.

4. **Create a budget and a marketing timeline**. Then execute and measure results—metrics matter. By establishing benchmarks you will be able to analyze what the Return On Investment (ROI) is on each marketing vehicle utilized. For example, if you are using a quick response (QR) code on a direct mail piece and the code is linked to a video, the metrics can be analyzed to assess how many times the video was viewed.

There are two distinct marketing techniques that can be utilized—traditional and digital—and I believe there is room and reason for both to co-exist in every marketing plan.

Traditional and digital marketing are complementary to each other. The trick to a successful marketing strategy is to identify what marketing tactics will produce the greatest results for your business without breaking your budget.

It is important to be clear where your target audience gets their information and market there. For example, if you are marketing to the age group of 25 – 40 years old, you may want to utilize digital marketing as your main channel of communication.

Each digital marketing channel has a further division of users based on demographics, so be mindful to select the correct digital medium for your target audience. For example, if your target audience is comprised of young mothers, and you are selling baby clothes, you most likely want to be marketing via Pinterest, as 80% of the demographics on that social site are women. If, however, your target audience is an older generation, a traditional marketing channel, which is not accessed online, may have a higher success rate.

Traditional marketing encompasses advertising through newspapers, magazines, direct mail, public relations, merchandising, sponsoring local events, television ads, tradeshow participation, bounce-back coupons and customer loyalty programs.

Newspapers, magazines and TV: Depending on your target audience, advertising in newspapers, magazines and television can be a viable strategy to market your product or service. The up-side is that you can reach large numbers of people. The down-side is that it can be very expensive and is a cluttered field, so at times it is hard to get noticed.

Direct mail: Items, such as postcards and even invitations, are considered direct mail. Some have deemed this method in the technological age as outdated. Despite USPS woes, I disagree. Online advertising is very noisy and direct mail offers a counter balance to this. Yes, we all receive a great deal of unsolicited mail. However, send a lumpy mail piece and I guarantee it won't get spammed out—and your message will get noticed! In my promotional products company, we send our clients big shiny red envelopes with gifts. We get noticed, and it drives profits.

Public relations (PR): Positive PR is great in raising awareness and creating credibility. If you have a breakthrough or newsworthy event that your target audience needs to know about, media is the way to go. Also, highlighting socially-conscious principles, donations or service efforts are a great way to leverage the availability of free press. PR can be expensive, but there are free options available. One option is to subscribe for free to a site, such as HARO, which stands for Help a Reporter Out. On this site, queries are posted providing an opportunity for you to contribute to a news story, raising brand awareness for your business. Another inexpensive online service providing publicity is PRWeb.com, which will release your business's latest news.

Merchandising: Of course, I must disclose that I am the President of an advertising specialty company, so I feel that giving a promotional product is a great marketing method to extend your brand. The promotional item need not be considered "trinkets and trash." The product chosen should match your intended recipient and reflect your brand and the event or reason for giving the product. The right product, given to the right people at the right time, can have lasting impact and drive profits.

Trade shows: Participating in a convention can be expensive if purchasing a booth, but not always. The benefit of a trade show is that it provides a highly targeted audience and offers the ability to build relationships through face-to-face contact. A trade show is efficient due to the high number of people you can reach in a short period of time. For a trade show to produce successful results, it is important that you create a specific plan to drive traffic to your booth (your promotional product specialist will help you with a plan) to develop solid leads.

Following up post-event by nurturing those leads will increase your conversion from prospect to profitable customer.

Bounceback coupons: I love bounceback coupons. It is simply a coupon that is given to your customer upon a purchase to encourage them to come back again. Bouncebacks are a great strategy as the results can be quantified and can also drive customers to try a new product line. For example, your favorite clothing store could offer a coupon to return for a discount on a shoe purchase.

If utilized, be sure to have a strong call-to-action, a time constraint (to create a sense of urgency) and a great offer. This strategy can be implemented in almost any industry— just be creative and watch your sales grow!

Customer loyalty programs: I have to be honest here. Does everyone need a customer loyalty program? NO.

I personally am annoyed by the fact that I now have a discount card for every single store I frequent in order to receive their discounts. Of course they are just tracking customer data (yeah, they should). However, from a consumer perspective— stop!

Some programs are artificial and we consumers know it. I know that my grocery store is hiking up the price and there is no real savings for me.

A counterpoint is Starbucks. Yes, it is a fact that I do enjoy my coffee—however, their program actually gives away free stuff, and I am loyal!

So, the moral of the story is: If you want to include a loyalty program in your marketing strategy, be sure you are actually providing a benefit to your customers or you may just end up annoying them.

Digital marketing is marketing where the outreach is online, such as through your website, sending electronic direct mail (EDM), social media marketing, video marketing, blogs and forums, mobile marketing, podcast and radio marketing, and utilizing QR codes in your program.

I am a big advocate of digital marketing, as it is a great equalizer for small businesses to compete with the big boys because of its low cost and availability.

A few of my favorite channels to extend your marketing message are:

Website: A website is the "shop," or the brick and mortar of your business, within the online community. It used to be merely an online brochure, but not anymore. A website communicates your product or service and brand identity to existing customers and prospects.

It can sell your products, or at the very minimum drive traffic through the sales funnel, culminating in sales.

To reiterate, your website must not be merely a brochure. To be a successful channel in a marketing plan it is important that the website drive people into or through the sales funnel by having a strong call-to-action inspiring people to take a step towards becoming a customer. For example, an effective website will have a capture page where visitors will give their information (name and email) in exchange for something of value to them (such as information or a discount on a service or product).

The capture page identifies people who are interested in what your business offers and is the beginning of developing a relationship with that prospect.

Electronic direct marketing: Sending a newsletter (content marketing) via email keeps your brand in front of your customers and is a great tool to relay information regarding your product or service. If done consistently, this method of outreach can produce great results and with minimal costs. With Constant Contact and other online sites, it has never been easier to inexpensively reach out to your customers.

Digital advertising: Also known as internet advertising, is the delivery of marketing messages to the target audience utilizing online channels, such as email marketing, social media, and through search engines. An example are the ads that appear as a result of keywords in your Google searches. Another great example of very targeted marketing are the ads that are presented along with your email (in Gmail they appear at the top of the page). These ads are delivered based on the content of the emails from your mailbox. This form of marketing, although it can culminate in a sale, is more about number of impressions and creating brand awareness.

Google Maps: Have a brick and mortar business? List your business on Google Maps for free and direct customers to your establishment.

Social media: For the right industry, this is an amazing tool that potentially affords you the ability to reach millions of people. There are many platforms to choose from. The most popular are Facebook, Twitter, LinkedIn, YouTube and Pinterest. Choose the platform where your target audience hangs out, and engage, educate, excite and evangelize your product or service for free.

You can also engage in pay-per-click (PPC) ad programs on social media, but you need to be very careful in how you execute a paid marketing plan to ensure a return on investment. See a PPC guru to ensure your plan produces the return you expect.

Video: Google loves video. Therefore when you post a video on a site, your marketing message moves up in ranking. According to a Comscore study, a customer who sees a video will stay on your site two minutes longer on average and is 64% more likely to purchase. It does not have to cost a fortune to create a video for your marketing plan.

Mobile marketing: Who doesn't have a multitude of mobile devices today? Providing information on the move is a reality, so all of your online marketing must be mobile-friendly— meaning that your web pages or advertisements are easily and quickly viewed on a mobile device.

Podcasts: A podcast is a series of audio and/or video content that is downloaded through the web. It is a convenient and inexpensive way to deliver your message to a very targeted audience who subscribe to your feed. Because it is subscription-based, it is efficient for your audience since they receive your new feeds automatically.

Radio: With more channels available today than ever before thanks to the Internet, this is a great medium. Although radio ads can be expensive, the reach is far and wide and they can be a great way to promote your business. Capitalize on this medium inexpensively by identifying opportunities to be a guest on a show.

QR codes: Yes, these are the funny-looking square codes that can be scanned with your phone, which then brings your target to an online site. They connect offline marketing, such as flyers, brochures and business cards, to the online world, moving your prospect into the sales funnel.

As mentioned above, they can also be used as a tool to measure marketing outreach by linking to a video (if you use bitly.com for your link, it will track how many people scan the code).

Use the QR code appropriately, however. I recently saw a QR code on a billboard—really? I'm going to jump out my car and scan that? Silly.

Also, just in case you think the black and white square code is ugly, custom codes (like my runner code in this book) are available at Customqrcodes.com.

Cross-marketing and strategic partnerships: This is often an overlooked, but extremely powerful, marketing tool for small business owners. A strategic partnership is an association with another entity with whom you share a common target audience. However, your businesses are not in direct competition. A pet groomer and a veterinarian, or a CPA and an insurance agent, are examples of partnerships in which you have the opportunity to cross-market.

Here are a few main points to help you focus on the execution of your marketing strategy:

1. Develop a plan and be sure your marketing message is relevant, relatable and timely. Understand what you want your marketing message to achieve, whether it is to create awareness, engage your targets, gain feedback or generate leads. Ultimately it is all about creating connections, nurturing those connections and converting them to profitable customers.

2. Whatever the matrix of tools in your marketing strategy, be sure that your message focuses on your target audience's challenges and your value proposition as the solution. Be consistent in your delivery.

3. People engage more easily if the message is framed in a story and is relevant and relatable to their needs. For example, if you are an investment advisor, sell your investments not on the technicalities of the fund but relay your message in a fashion that engages your target in an emotional way by explaining how the fund will provide security for them and their family. Review

Chris Westfall's advice as to how to make an impactful message in chapter two.

4. The timing of your message is also important. Most people begin to market when they become slow in the office. Marketing must be done consistently in busy times and slow times; but also be cognizant of when your target audience will be more receptive. For example, marketing for new tax clients on April 16 is not great timing. Nobody wants to think about hiring a CPA the day after taxes are due! A better time would be the last quarter, when businesses and individuals begin year-end planning.

5. Make sure you can deliver on your promise. Okay, I feel compelled to advise that your message must be in alignment with the promise you deliver. Do <u>not</u> market a promise upon which you cannot deliver. Underestimating and over-delivering will keep your customers coming back.

   In addition, be sure that your infrastructure can support the influx of sales post-marketing. Not being able to fulfill post-marketing can spell disaster—just ask those entrepreneurs that hit the jackpot with the Oprah effect and then failed miserably. Their product was featured on her show, sales skyrockets beyond what the infrastructure could support and they were out of business before they were really in business!

6. Following up is key in realizing the ROI on your marketing strategy. Review the metrics on every campaign and follow up. For example, if you choose to use electronic direct marketing, perhaps by utilizing Constant Contact, look at the analytics. The analytics are your gold. Those individuals who have clicked through to your website or responded in some way to your call-to-action need a follow up email or call. You must take action to reel in the results.

Also, watching your analytics will guide you as to where to focus your marketing efforts, which will ultimately save you wasted dollars on channels that are not producing. Marketing doesn't have to cost you a fortune if you are strategic and watch your analytics.

PILLAR #3 – Sales

No sales, no profits, no business. Marketing is the heartbeat of your business, but in order for your business to thrive, you must also have a rock-solid sales process.

Marketing is about identifying your customer needs and communicating your product or service as the solution to their needs.

Sales is about convincing your prospects that you have the answer and converting those prospects into profitable customers.

Your marketing efforts will create awareness of your product or service and attract prospective customers who will then enter the sales funnel. A *sales funnel* is the process of moving your prospect from initial contact to final sale. As you move your contacts through each step in the process, barriers to the sale are removed until the sale is completed.

The stages are as follows:

Generating leads – A lead is developed as a result of your marketing efforts. But, not all leads are created equal. When a business is first launched, it is easy to pursue every lead that is generated with abandon. However, this is not the direct path to a sale.

Evaluate whether your lead meets your very specific customer profile. Only if your lead matches your target customer profile should you then pursue the prospect and move them into the next step of the sales funnel.

Pay attention to which marketing source your most fruitful leads are derived from and leverage the sources that are most productive.

Prospecting – At this stage, a lead enters the sales funnel and typically has had a conversation about your product or service and it has been established that your offer is a match to their need. Every lead must be deserving of space in your sales funnel or they are just wasting precious time and resources. The next very important step is the qualification process.

Qualifying the prospect – When we select less-than-ideal prospects, we waste time, which always equates to money. The goal in the qualification process is to establish which prospects are the best match to your offer, have the most promise of converting to customers as quickly as possible, and deserve your time and energy.

The qualification process is solely focused on your prospect and not on your product or service. Through continued conversation you will:

- Verify that the prospect has the need and sees value in your solution.
- Establish that the prospect is the decision-maker or has direct access to the decision-maker.
- Confirm that there are appropriated funds and a timeline attached to the sale.

This process can be lengthy and may take several points of contact to complete.

Converting a prospect to a customer – This is the process of cultivating relationships and nurturing your prospects into profitable customers. Conversion is the result of developing your customers through understanding their challenges better than they do, effectively articulating your value proposition and guiding them to view your product or service as the only solution to their challenge.

That is the basic framework of the sales process. The above steps clearly define the process, but let's talk about sales today in our hyper-competitive technology-based market and how the sales funnel has changed. Today, purchasing agents and procurement teams are trained and armed with data. You, the sales representative of your product or service, are no longer considered the source of information that provides the solutions to your customer's challenges. Thanks to technology and the availability of information, solutions are easily identified, benefit analyses extrapolated and prices compared—way before the sales rep walks through the door.

So, while you still need to generate leads via your marketing buzz and turn leads into qualified prospects, the conversion process has really changed. Thanks to the Internet many offerings have been commoditized, making it important that your conversion methodology relies on selling value and not just price.

Gone are the good old days of solution-based selling. For business-to-business (B2B) or businesses-to-consumer (B2C) companies, selling is no longer the process of merely identifying a prospect with a problem to which you offer the solution and selling them your solution.

Thanks to the ease of gaining knowledge, our sophisticated prospects come to the salespeople fully-loaded with information.

So, for you to be successful in converting your prospect to a customer, you must be rock-solid in your ability to build a relationship with your prospect. This means in order to sell based on value; the salesperson needs to be a terrific communicator.

A high level of communication begins with listening. A great listener will have the ability to discern information and identify the true needs of the prospect beyond what they have articulated. They will communicate effectively the value the prospect will gain by choosing your product or service as the solution. Value-based selling is all about understanding your customer's challenges better than they understand themselves, building trust and speaking their language.

To sell based on value and increase your conversion rates, frame your conversation as follows:

1. Identify how your offering will truly impact your customer. Why does your customer have to have it? Is the customer's core need to save time (which translates into money) or is it to ensure quality (translates into money)? Identify what their true desire is and pivot your conversation away from price and to the real value they are searching for.

2. Communicate with your prospect in a consultative fashion. This requires that your conversation focus on assessing the needs of your customer and being able to effectively articulate why your offer is the clear choice to meet their needs. Guide your client through the decision process and present why your company's core strengths, service or product will benefit them.

By approaching your potential customer as a consultant-advisor and relaying the fact that your expertise will greatly benefit them, you will build trust—and trust is the cornerstone to converting a prospect into a loyal customer.

3. Recognize the importance of timing your outreach prior to when your target "has to have it." Just like the timing of your marketing message, be aware of changes within your target market's industry as well as external pressures, such as new government regulations, that will create a need.

    Identifying unrecognized needs—prior to your customer—creates opportunity for you to proactively provide compelling solutions to their needs. If a salesperson engages the prospect with a consultative conversation prior to the time the prospect really needs the solution, the outcome will result in a quicker conversion to a loyal customer.

    For example, I had a client who provides consulting services in the healthcare field and began marketing and conversing with her customers and prospects about the impact and solutions to Obamacare well in advance of the implementation of the new healthcare program. My client responded quickly and by doing so was viewed by her target market as the expert and the only solution to their challenge. Her timing, along with her expertise, increased her business exponentially.

Being ahead of the game is an advantage. However, there is always a way to redirect the conversation to value. For example, businesses are frequently asked to participate in a Request For Proposal (RFP). An RFP, in my opinion, is equivalent to a price war. But there is a way to pivot an RFP to your advantage if your business can provide a better solution than what is being requested in the RFP.

The strategy is to offer a proposal for what they have specifically requested in the RFP but also to give them an alternate option that is a creative and, of course, better option. Encourage your prospect to think differently and turn the table a bit—by doing so you have created an opportunity to demonstrate your expertise and creativity. The result can inspire the company to drop all other bidders and go with your solution.

An additional channel to drive sales conversations is through social media. An online presence drives sales indirectly through exposure and brand awareness. If, however, your engagement in social media is done with a specific strategy (and part of an overall marketing strategy), social media can directly create sales.

For business-to-business sales, the undisputed social media front-runner in driving sales is LinkedIn for prospecting and targeting conversations to the decision-makers in your audience. Kurt Shaver is the foremost expert on leveraging

LinkedIn as a marketing and sales tool and is our contributing sales author.

Kurt Shaver is Founder of The Sales Foundry, a LinkedIn Sales Solutions Channel Partner specializing in social selling skills training. He offers our readers a free social selling resource, including a two-minute LinkedIn Sales Score at www.salesfoundry.com.

Contribution from LinkedIn Sales Expert Kurt Shaver

The Internet has given rise to social media applications like LinkedIn, Facebook and Twitter, which have changed the way the world communicates. That includes Business-to-Business (B2B) buyers.

As more B2B buyers rely on social channels for decision-making information, salespeople need to participate in these channels early in the sales cycle. While each application has it strengths, LinkedIn is the undisputed leader when it comes to winning new clients in B2B markets.

Following are 10 tips for increasing your results from four key areas of LinkedIn.

Build a Professional Profile

1. **Do You Get the Picture?** Have a head shot that conveys the image that you want your customers to have of you. No full body or waist-up photos, no family members or pets, and no photos of you winning the tequila drinking contest in Cabo unless you are Sammy Hagar and tequila is your BUSINESS.

2. **It's a Headline, Not (Just) Your Title.** The majority of people just display their title in the "Headline" area right under their name (i.e. VP of HR, Account Executive, IT Administrator). That is a waste of precious branding "real-estate." The Headline section allows for 120 characters. Use them all for an attention-grabbing, customer-oriented benefit statement. The goal is to attract click-throughs from prospective customers when they see your profile on a list with other profiles.

Grow Your Network

3. **Connection Direction.** When people start on LinkedIn, they often wonder who they should invite to reach the coveted "500+" level. It is recommended to invite people whom you have known in a business setting or might have the possibility for a mutually beneficial business relationship in the future. Some areas to look for Connections include:

- Customers
- Prospects
- Co-workers
- Suppliers
- Referral partners
- Past referrers or referees
- Friends and family (if a business context exists)
- Networking groups (offline and online)

4. **Invite with Distinction.** Have you ever received a LinkedIn invitation and wondered, "Who is this person and why are they inviting me to connect?" If so, chances are they sent the default invitation that everyone else does—I'd like to add you to my professional network on LinkedIn. Don't be that guy.

   Follow this 3-step process and you will distinguish yourself from the crowd:

   - Establish context and build rapport
   - Position your value to your customers
   - Close with a call to action

   Here is an example that will impress, rather than confuse, the receiver—and it only took 28 seconds to type:

   "It was good to meet you at the marketing conference. Your company's growth is impressive. I help growing companies find and retain top talent. Please accept my invitation and let's see how we can help each other."

5. **Accept and Reply.** When you receive a LinkedIn invitation, don't just click the Accept button and move on. LinkedIn pops up the option to "Send a Message." Since Connections are all about relationships, this is the ideal time to write a short reply to strengthen that relationship. A short question is great for continuing a conversation. Here is an example of a reply that could spark further dialog:

"Thanks for the invitation to connect. I see we are both in the Advertising business. What areas do you focus on?"

Find New Prospects

6. **Desperately Seeking Prospects.** The most powerful prospecting feature of LinkedIn is the Advanced Search where you can filter through more than 250M+ members based on characteristics like Title, Company, Location, Industry and Keywords. The final and most important criteria for prospecting is to filter by Relationship=2nd Connections. This increases the chances that one of your Level 1 Connections can introduce you.

7. **Get Free Leads Emailed to You.** Do you know about Saved Searches? It's a feature that lets you save search criteria so LinkedIn keeps looking for people who fit the criteria. You can choose to have LinkedIn email you the fresh leads every week. It's like Google Alerts, except for people on LinkedIn. If you set up a saved search for CFOs in the Financial Services industry within 50 miles of Chicago and a new person gets promoted into that position tomorrow, LinkedIn will let you know by the end of the week.

8. **Follow Target Companies.** Have you identified some companies that you would like as customers? Search for their LinkedIn Company Page and Follow it. You will receive company news in your LinkedIn Home Page feed to help you discover trigger events like new hires, acquisitions or new products or

services. Even if you miss the news on your Home Page, you can quickly navigate back to the Company Page of companies that you are following.

Engage Your Network

9. **Become a Groupie.** LinkedIn has almost three million Groups arranged by job titles, departments, functions, industries, locations, companies, schools and more. Groups provide opportunities to get answers or give them. You can poll your prospects for quick, inexpensive market research or add your expertise to a discussion. Add value, and your visibility and value as a subject matter expert, will rise.

10. **Curate, Don't Create.** Most people are too busy or not trained to produce a steady stream of content to share with their network. Don't worry. It is much easier to play Editor and just select other people's content to share. As long as it is important to your network, your value as a trusted resource will rise. Find content on your company web site, industry news sites and the social web.

I recommend that you create a plan of action to utilize the information that Kurt has provided to increase your sales and outperform your competition. LinkedIn is an effective networking tool, and I can attest that I have reaped the rewards of including this platform in my sales and marketing strategy.

We will discuss metrics more thoroughly in chapter seven. However, note that it is important to track your sales success rates.

Analyze your marketing-to-lead rate. This will identify marketing channels that are performing and which are dogs.

Identify what your lead-to-qualified-prospect rate is. This will establish if your marketing efforts are hitting your segmented targets. What is your prospect-to-rock-star-profitable-customer rate?

Evaluate your sales method and identify weaknesses in your tactics and leverage your strengths. If you don't measure your success, how will you know if you are winning?

Also, don't let fear stop you from going after sales. Taking action and going after your customers is the only way to succeed. Customers will not beat a path to your door, unless you are Apple and introducing the latest and greatest product.

If you have identified and qualified a prospect, go get them! The bigger the customer, the bigger your effort needs to be. I once identified a client whom I thought had the potential to be a great client for my business. I had a few conversations with them, did one small project and then decided I wanted all their projects, so I requested a short meeting to introduce myself in person.

I knew that I would gain more information about their needs and build trust in my business's ability to provide solutions for them better with a personal visit. Nothing ever beats a face-to-face conversation. They agreed to a thirty minute meeting the following Tuesday. The issue? They were four planes away. Not a problem—my first flight was at 6:03a.m. out of Albany, NY and by gosh I was in Lexington, KY by 11:30a.m. for my meeting. Two flights home, back in at 11:30p.m., and the rest is millions of dollars of history. Go get 'em!

PILLAR# 4 – Customer Service and Developing Passionate Fans

The key driver to the success of your business is developing overly zealous, enthusiastic, impassioned fans that will spread the good word about your product or service. Again, think Apple devotees.

Your fans are the golden nuggets to sales growth via referrals. There are always going to be naysayers, and then there are the neutral uncommitted fence sitters, but to create a stellar business you need fans and lots of them!

Referrals are, quite frankly, the best marketing you can get for your business. Word of mouth testimonies will drive people to flock to your door.

Think about the great new French restaurant that opens in town. It doesn't take long for word to spread, does it?

You don't have to wait for the word to spread organically. You can nudge the referral out of your customer.

Many times, it just doesn't cross a customer's mind to refer you or your business, so just simply ask them "I love working with you. Do you know anyone who is very similar to you whom I can also service?"

You have told them you enjoy working with them and want customers like them, so chances are they will give you a few good leads.

Another tactic is to remind your customers to post testimonials on your website or give them directly to you to be used in your marketing materials. You can also reward those who refer with a referral fee, a 10% off coupon, free dessert…whatever works.

In the end, always, always, always thank your referrals. Personally, I still hand-write notes. I have a stack on my desk, and typically I write a note of gratitude on a daily basis.

So, how do we create zillions of passionate fans? Amazing customer service.

Here I've brought to you **customer service expert Shep Hyken** to weigh in on the subject. Shep is a *New York Times* and *Wall Street Journal* bestselling author and renowned customer service expert. His most recent book, *Amaze Every Customer Every Time: 52 Tools for Delivering the Most Amazing Customer Service on the Planet*, is another bestseller and a must in every small business's library. (Find Shep's book online at chrisvanderzyden.com/AmazeEveryCustomer.)

Here are Shep's tips to deliver amazing customer service and ensure that your customers not only keep coming back but also refer you to the world!

Contribution from Bestselling Author and
Renowned Customer Service Expert Shep Hyken

How to Deliver an Amazing Customer Service Experience

An amazing customer service experience comes down to this: Sell a product or service that works and be nice to the customer about it. It's that simple. I could stop there, as most people would agree with that statement. However, this is just "what it is"—not how to do it.

Understanding "what it is" becomes the starting point. Knowing "how to do it" and actually doing it (customer service) is the execution. The result can be any one or all of the following:

1. Happier customers

2. More loyalty, which means more sales from existing customers (frequency of purchases)

3. Higher sales per transaction (higher average sale)

4. Word-of-mouth referrals from happy customers (your evangelists)

5. Happier employees (a customer service-focused company usually is also employee-focused)

6. Lower employee turnover (employees are happier— more fulfilled—and don't leave)

7. Price becomes less relevant

8. Set you ahead of competitors who may have similar (or even better) products but offer less service

9. Reputation—people want to buy from you and people want to work for you

10. Profit—more money to the bottom line

And who wouldn't want those results?

So, how to deliver amazing customer service? Well, I've written a number of books and hundreds of articles, this being yet another. In honor of the first year anniversary of the book, I compiled a list of 40 short tips that will help just about any company deliver amazing customer service.

40 Quick Tips to Deliver a Better Customer Service Experience

1. Manage first impressions. They set the tone.
2. Manage last impressions. They create "lasting" impressions.
3. Show up on time. Being late is a sign of disrespect to the people waiting.
4. Always do your best.
5. Smile. It's better than a frown or an expression of apathy.
6. Be accountable. Don't blame others, and accept responsibility.
7. If a problem comes your way, you own it, even if it is not your department.
8. Even if you own the problem (see # 7) and you do have to pass it on to someone else, circle back with the customer to make sure it has been resolved.
9. Show up early.
10. Stay late.
11. Do more than is expected.
12. Under-promise and over-deliver.
13. Be proactive.
14. Build rapport.

15. Aim for perfection, even if it is not a reality.

16. If there is a problem, respond quickly.

17. Return calls quickly.

18. Care! Don't just act like you care. Really care!

19. Be enthusiastic.

20. Always say, "Thank you."

21. Leave personal problems at home.

22. If you have to transfer a customer to another person, make sure it's the right person.

23. If you have to transfer a customer to another person, make sure they are there.

24. Treat your colleagues at work the way you know the customer should be treated.

25. Pretend the customer is a member and make them know they are special and doing business with a place that is special.

26. Customer loyalty is about the next time—every time. What are you doing now to make sure the customer comes back next time?

27. Customer loyalty is great. Partnership is even better. How can you be your customer's partner?

28. When it comes to customer service, you can be a leader. Set the example and show your colleagues what great customer service is all about.

29. The customer is not always right, but they are always the customer. Always treat them with respect, even if they are wrong.

30. It's okay to disagree as long as you aren't disagreeable.

31. Sometimes you have to say, "No." When you do, be polite and do it with tact and respect.

32. Don't make business personal. Usually, customers are mad at a situation or the company, not at you personally. You have the power to make it better or worse based on how you respond.

33. If you don't have an answer, admit it. Then go find the answer and report back. Don't make up something because it sounds right.

34. Avoid using company or industry jargon that the customer might not be familiar with.

35. Never lie.

36. Recognize your awesome responsibility. At any time, to the customer you are dealing with, you are the company: the name, brand, reputation, etc.

37. Don't copy someone else's customer service strategy. Then you are just the same. Take what someone else has done and make it better—make it your own.

38. Answer the phone within three rings. Two is better.

39. Avoid putting people on hold for more than 30 seconds. It seems like a lot longer.

40. Don't offer new customers something you wouldn't offer your loyal customers (or at least something of comparable value).

BONUS: Always say, "Thank you."

These tips may be simple, but they are powerful. And as simple as they seem in theory, practical application may be more difficult. The key is to apply these (and any other ideas you may want to add to the list) on a consistent basis. The best companies aren't great some of the time. They are great all of the time. That's customer amazement. And, another reminder... Being amazing is simply being better than average—all of the time. So, be amazing!

There will be glitches in your business. What happens when there is an error? For example, the delivery is not what the customer expected. How a business reacts when posed with a situation that goes horribly wrong displays their level of customer service and the character of their business, and can have the greatest impact on your referrals and repeat business.

It is inevitable that at times something will go wrong. There are a myriad of reasons that business fail in their delivery. Some are controllable and some not, but the business can always—and I mean absolutely unequivocally always—control how they respond.

A positive, quick "We'll take care of it," and then action to take care of the issue will gain trust and loyalty. Respond quickly and positively and turn a failure into an opportunity to prove your high-level service and win customers in the face of difficulty.

PILLAR #5 – Finances

Accounting {ac-count-ing}: The process of identifying, measuring and communicating economic information to permit informed judgment and decisions by users of the financial information.

Yes, this is the part of owning a business that everyone would like to dismiss, but unfortunately every taxing authority won't let you forget.

I know, accounting is just not sexy like marketing and sales. It isn't fun, and is downright a necessary evil. I feel your pain. Yes, I have a CPA license, and even I do not enjoy the financial part of business, except for knowing how profitable my businesses are!

The fact of the matter, however, is that the knowledge we gain from financials is our premier business tool as we strategize and make good management decisions.

If you are starting a business and your expertise is not in the finance world, hire a Certified Public Accountant to set up your accounting system. I understand that with all of the resources available it is tempting to go it alone thinking you will save money, but this is an area that has grave consequences if not done correctly, and can cost you dearly.

Your accounting must be set up correctly to ensure that you are in compliance with all tax regulations. Your CPA will ultimately save you time and money, and will continuously advise and strategize with you as you grow your business.

A few guidelines as to how to identify a CPA who is right for you and your business:

- Be sure they are licensed and designated as an active CPA to practice in the state in which you are registered to do business.

  Get recommendations from trusted resources, your attorney, insurance agent or banker. Assess if the CPA has the experience that matches your business.

  Contrary to popular opinion, not all CPAs are created alike; just like any other profession, there are specialties within the industry. It is important that you feel comfortable and trust your CPA implicitly, as they will be intimately aware of your financial situation and will be one of the resources you depend upon the most.

- Be prepared to divulge all of your plans and documents when you meet with the CPA. Go into your meeting armed with your business plan and as much support as possible to get the full benefit of your CPA's expertise.

Your CPA will guide you in setting up an accounting system that is right for your business. He or she will determine if you should be reporting on a *cash basis* (income is recognized when received and expenses when paid) or *accrual basis* (income is recognized when earned and expenses when incurred), or you may qualify for a modified accrual system.

Your CPA will help set up a bookkeeping system. There are many software programs available. However, QuickBooks is a very intuitive system that I recommend.

A bookkeeper is responsible for recording the day-to-day transactions of your business, such as invoicing your customers and paying your vendors. The bookkeeper reports to you, the owner, and as a business owner it is your responsibility to be intimately involved with the finances of your business and understand your assets, liabilities and the equity.

Every successful entrepreneur utilizes their financial statements to gauge the profitability of the business and make strategic decisions as they move towards fulfilling the vision, goals and objectives of the organization.

I have watched too many business owners who kept their head in the sand in regards to their business's financial position and, as a result, have failed, or at the very least did not reach their full potential.

It is critical that you understand and engage in the financial management of your business. If trouble is brewing, your financials will tell you and will allow you to be proactive in your management decisions to counteract the problems.

So get a cup of coffee, go for a run, do whatever it takes to energize yourself and take this information in—if you are to be a successful business owner this information is critical!!

The basics of understanding the financial picture of your business are as follows:

Balance sheet – The balance sheet is a picture of the position of a company at a specific date. It provides the cost basis of assets, liabilities and owner's equity. The *assets* represent what resources a business owns and are intended to provide a future benefit, such as cash, accounts receivable, inventory, land, buildings, goodwill and investments. A *liability* is an obligation of the business, such as loans, accounts payable and accrued liabilities. *Owner's equity* represents the amount invested into the company by the stockholders plus accumulated profits of the business and is made up of paid-in-capital, common stock and retained earnings. The owner's equity is computed by subtracting the liabilities from assets.

Here is a guide to reading your balance sheet:

- The balance sheet provides the reader with information needed to determine the level of solvency and liquidity for a company.
- A key indicator to liquidity is the current ratio, or the ratio of current assets to current liabilities.
- Current assets, such as accounts receivable, are those assets that can be converted to cash within the current period.
- Current liabilities, such as accounts payable, are those liabilities that are expected to be paid off within a current period. A 2:1 ratio (twice the assets as liabilities) is a good marker of a healthy small business.

A review of the amount of debt on the balance sheet in comparison to equity is an indicator of solvency. Of course, the ideal is to have equity outweigh debt.

A few other key ratios to analyze that will provide an indicator as to how well the inventory and receivables are being managed are:

- **Inventory turnover** is the number of times that inventory is replaced in a period. This ratio is computed by dividing the cost of goods sold (from the income statement) by average inventory in a given period. This ratio is an indicator of inventory management. If the ratio is high, this means inventory is being depleted at an acceptable rate. A lower level means inventory is not turning as quickly and may be overstocked. The goal is for inventory to keep pace with demand by your customers. A comparison from year-to-year will give an idea as to changes in performance.

- **Receivable turnover** computes how many times a business collects receivables in a period. It is computed by dividing credit sales by average accounts receivable. The higher the ratio the better. If, over a period of time, your analysis indicates a lower ratio this may highlight a collection issue.

Income Statement – This is the statement that typically gets all the focus, as it provides a measurement of your profit or loss. It displays all of your revenue sources and your expenses for a given period of time. It encapsulates your gross sales, cost of goods sold, operating expenses and depreciation.

The first indicator of health on the income statement is to assess its *gross profit margin*. This will answer the very basic question as to whether or not you are making a profit on the products you are selling. It is calculated by subtracting the cost of goods sold from sales and dividing by sales revenue. Obviously, the higher the margin the better.

The second measurement to analyze is the *operating profit margin*. This will indicate how well the company is operating. It is computed by subtracting day-to-day operating expenses from revenue to indicate operating earnings. Dividing operating earnings from revenue will provide the operating profit margin. Again, the higher the better.

Finally, the end game: *net profit margin*. Net income divided by revenue will measure how much income is derived from every dollar of revenue.

I also recommend drilling into operating expenses to expose any out of line increase in specific expenses.

When reviewing an income statement for an established business it is helpful to compare with previous years to identify trends.

Statement of Cash Flow – This document shows the cash flowing in and out of a business and is a conversion of an accrual basis income statement to cash basis in order to give a true picture of the health of a business. This is a great analytical tool as it indicates the company's ability to pay bills and as well as its overall viability. This statement is divided into three parts: operations, investing and financing.

- *Operations cash flow* is derived from day-to-day operation of the business. This portion monitors movement of funds from operations and includes movement of accounts payable and accounts receivable.
- *Investing cash flow* includes cash movement for the purchase or sale of long-term assets, such as equipment.
- *Financing* includes all long-term borrowing or repayment of debt.

It is possible to have a profit yet a negative cash flow. Why?

Cash withdrawn from the business that is not included as an expense on the income statement, such as owner's draws, flows out of a business and can create a negative cash flow. For example, if you take out a loan it does not appear as an expense on the income statement, as it is an owner transaction and impacts only the balance sheet.

Conversely when you pay the money back into the business it is not shown as income, but as a loan repayment, again this does not impact the income statement.

So while you may show a profit on your income statement, your cash flow can in fact still be negative.

Typically, the income statement and cash flow are reviewed together. The cash flow statement indicates how healthy your business is—ideally the profit on the income statement will reflect that cash flowing in on the cash flow statement.

While a company is in start-up mode this may not be true, as there may be large investment in inventory and a lag in payments from receivables. In time, this will even out.

At the beginning of a business, or if you have a business that has a long production and payment lead time, cash management is really important as you bridge the investment into the business with the customer payments.

A few strategies to consider managing your cash flow better:

- *Profit margins*: Focus your attention on selling higher margin items or introducing higher margin items into your product line.
- *Inventory management*: Stay on top of your inventory ratios and be proactive in adjusting inventory levels as needed.
- *Increase controls on cash management*: Negotiate longer terms with your bankers and suppliers in order to hold cash longer. Always pay your vendors on time and within terms, but do not pay them early. Hold your cash.
- *Oversee operating expenses*: Do not become complacent in your reoccurring expenses. Shop for the best rates for insurance, utilities, telephone, etc.
- *Decrease your accounts receivable collection time*: Reward early payers with a discount (i.e. 2%, net 10 terms), and for those slow payers encourage them to pay on

time by instituting a finance charge for over-term offenders.

Budgeting:

There are many benefits to creating an annual budget. Doing so:

1. Identifies strengths and weaknesses of various segments within the organization by comparing forecasted expectations with actual numbers.

2. Provides an opportunity to assess the assumptions of the business, including why it exists in the current business environment and how well the business is performing in relation to the competitive market. Like the SWOT analysis in business planning, budgeting requires that you look for opportunities and threats annually.

3. Requires specific planning for the future and evaluation of the success and failures of every aspect of the business.

4. Establishes benchmarks for employees and encourages them to meet their goals. It is also used as a tool to evaluate the performance of all contributors to the finances of the business.

The ultimate value in budgeting is that it forces a business to look ahead, project and forecast where the business is anticipated to be in the future. For small business owners, it is easy to get stuck *working in* the business, as opposed to *working on* the business.

When time is spent focusing on the long-term planning of a business, that is when real growth occurs. Budgeting not only forces a look into the future but also forces a review of actual numbers and assessment of past performance.

So, the most valuable part of budgeting is the reality check as to what is working and what is not, and this is the first step to creating the necessary change to move your business to a higher level.

Larger companies will review and reforecast on a quarterly basis. For a small business, I recommend reviewing an annual budget monthly.

The Process of Budgeting:

Budget both your balance sheet and your income statement. There is a tendency to just focus on the income statement and expenses; however, if you are a start-up and are projecting growth it is necessary to budget increases in inventory, capital expenditures and the impact on cash flow.

Step 1- Make realistic assumptions about your business.

How much income can be derived from sales of your product or service? Analyze the market and competition, and estimate how much of the market can be captured. Assess how much the structure of the business is capable of producing.

If the business is selling a product, how much will it cost to produce the product and how much inventory will be needed?

The cost is the estimate of cost of goods sold—actual costs to produce an item.

What are the operating expenses estimated to be? Forecast both variable and fixed costs month-by-month. Variable costs, such as material, are expenses that vary dependent on production volume. Fixed costs, such as rent, remain the same regardless of production level.

If there are employees, what will the payroll burden be, including taxes?

Based on the structure of the company, what is the projected tax rate? Review the tax estimates with your CPA.

What capital expenditures are anticipated? Bid all capital expenditures out to get as accurate a projection as possible.

Also be sure to budget any debt service. This is often overlooked—however, payments required for debt taken on to start your business must be budgeted.

Step 2 - Create your budget.

This does not have to be a long, drawn-out process. Simply review the historical information and compare it to the projections and ask yourself "Does this make sense?" If you are a start-up and have no historical data, begin the budget based on projections as researched when assessing your business model.

Create the budget by utilizing your accounting software or do it manually.

Review the budget monthly and investigate any discrepancies. Too often a business owner will make up a budget and then file it away never to be utilized. The budget is a financial tool and, when analyzed, will provide guidance as to what adjustments are needed in management decisions to better meet the budget and grow profits.

A final accounting note…guidance on internal accounting controls. Far too often we hear about a small business that suffered because of employee theft. Strong internal controls that can protect your business from theft will create efficiencies and ensure accuracy in how you operate your business.

There are five areas of control:

1. **Segregation of Duties** – Divide accounting duties so that one individual is not able to make a mistake that will not be caught. In essence, a system of checks and balances will ensure accuracy and guard against impropriety. Any person who has physical access to cash should not be involved in recording transactions. For example, the person who receives cash or checks for service and makes the deposit should not also be responsible for recording the transaction in the records.

   In a small business, it is sometimes hard to have adequate separation of duties because of the small number of employees. In this case, the owner needs to step up and oversee certain aspects to ensure separation. For example, the person who reconciles the bank accounts should not be the same person who is responsible for cash receipts or disbursements. In this circumstance, the owner, outside bookkeeper or CPA should reconcile the monthly bank statements.

2. **Restricted Access** – This guidance pertains to the restriction of physical inventory access to personnel who are authorized to move inventory. Also, unused physical checks should be secured.

3. **Document Controls** – All documents such as checks, sales invoices, customer receipts, shipping documents, purchase orders and receiving reports should be pre-numbered. This will provide an audit trail and also will ensure that all transactions are captured within your system.

4. **Processing Controls** – These are procedures that are set up to ensure that all documents are processed correctly. For example, cash receipts for the day are totaled and the machine tape of total remittances is compared to the amounts recognized in the deposit and accounts receivable/sales ledger. Another example is the comparison of purchase orders to vendors' invoices to ensure accuracy.

5. **Reconciliation Controls** – This is the process of reconciling the subsidiary ledgers to the general ledger. Accounts receivable, accounts payable, inventory,

property and equipment are commonly reconciled in addition to the bank accounts. Again, if you are a business owner with just a few staff members, you should reconcile the bank statements every month.

As a business owner, you must review your financial statements monthly and perform spot checks of records periodically.

PILLAR #6 – Creating a Team

"I hire people brighter than me, and then I get out of their way."

~ Lee Iacocca

I love this quote—hire people who are smarter than you for whatever capacity they are meant to fill. Your business is growing and now you think you need to hire help. But you are reticent because you think, "What if the business doesn't continue to grow?" Or perhaps the business is seasonal and the need for employees is not easy to project.

How do you know when it is time to hire a team to support you? When it is evident that the business cannot grow without gaining additional expertise, or support is needed to allow you to focus on your core strengths.

For many business owners, the threshold is when you are not spending at least 80% of your time on income-producing activities.

Hiring is tricky. You don't want to hire too many people and end up having to do layoffs. And on the flip side, you don't want to not hire and risk burning out your existing workers with overtime.

In addition, most business owners want to ensure that they have the necessary skills in-house to service their existing customers and have room to grow and take on more work.

Here are a few pointers to hiring a stellar team:

1. Identify the areas of the business you need help with. Are there tasks you are doing that simply need to be delegated? Or do you need additional expertise that you don't have in order to grow your business? Write a list of all the areas that need to be supported and use that as your organizational chart of team members.

2. Write a detailed job description and salary for each position. This description will be your guide as you go through the hiring process and determine if the candidate's skills match your needs. The job description also provides a clear list of responsibilities by which to assess performance.

3. Identify ideal candidates and interview. Those that pass the interview test must be screened. Check references and perform background checks—and do not skip this. Another little piece of advice; do not hire family and friends because they are cheap and easily identified. This frequently ends in disaster.

4. Create a system of training and motivating employees to ensure they are productive, happy, achieving team

members so that you retain them. Great employees can be hard to find, and it is an expensive and time-consuming process, so do whatever you can to ensure your team members stay put.

5. Consider incentivizing your employees with a profit-sharing plan or some tie to revenue sharing. It is amazing how the level of performance can dramatically rise if proper incentives are put into place.

6. Many times in a small business there is a concern, especially if the position is a sales position, that the employee whom you have invested a great deal of time into training will jump ship to another company and, worst-case scenario, take business with them. If you are really worried, have them sign a non-compete agreement. And be sure that you are supporting your people as much as possible in their drive for success.

If a full-time employee is not the answer for your business, there are many other options to gain assistance:

Virtual assistants are great for specific projects like database entry, online research, managing email, scheduling and even vetting out new business. Elance is a popular site to source online employment.

Temporary staffing agencies are great if you are uneasy about needing full-time help as you grow. It is also a great way to try out a new employee prior to committing to a full-time hire.

Internships or work/study programs with local colleges or high schools can also be a great resource for temporary help.

Independent contractors are a great way to gain expertise without the full economic burden of an employee. You will save on having to pay for benefits, office space and equipment, not to mention saving on payroll taxes. Being a CPA, I must emphasize that whomever you hire as an independent contractor must meet all three main Internal Revenue tests of an independent contractor:

1. The company must have no behavioral control over the independent contractor. The contractor must have control over how, when and where they perform their service and what equipment and supplies they utilize to perform the job.

2. The company should not control the business aspects of the contractor, including the extent to which the contractor can market services to other opportunities; and the contractor cannot be guaranteed a regular "wage" amount.

3. The type of relationship must meet all requirements of independence, such as a written contract and lack of any employee-type benefits. Also, the relationship must not be permanent.

There are very specific guidelines under each of the three categories, and if you are in doubt as to whether the relationship qualifies as an independent contractor, consult your CPA. If it is deemed that they do not meet the requirements of an independent contractor, you may be held liable for employment taxes and penalties.

PILLAR #7 – Technology

The advancement of technology is one of the most compelling reasons as to why it is easier to create a profitable and successful business now more so than ever before.

If you are old enough, you will remember when the first fax machine was introduced to the mass market. A business owner spent thousands of dollars for the ability to transmit information over the telephone wire!

Today we rarely fax thanks to scanning and emailing, but if we did a fax machine is inexpensive today. This is just one example of many as to how the advancement of technology has leveled the playing field as to who can enter the world of entrepreneurship and be a successful business owner. People are no longer required to have a fortune behind them to launch a business.

In addition to the fact that the cost of technology has been contained, technology has also created amazing efficiencies.

Today we have the advantage of an array of software, apps and the Internet that contribute enormously to the ease in developing a profitable business. Gone are the days when you painstakingly had to sit on the sidelines waiting for feedback from your customers or information from key players on a project.

We have instant connectivity through email and instant messaging and social media platforms. We have project management that is housed in the cloud that every team member has continuous access to. We no longer are required to fly to a meeting, thanks to Skype, GoToMeeting and other videoconferencing options.

Our accounting is more streamlined than ever thanks to software packages. A customer relationship management system (CRM) used to be enormously expensive, but now we have a multitude of CRM system available for less than a thousand dollars.

Our advancing technology affords us greater ease and minimal cost to creating a profitable business.

What does this mean? These enormous resources save time and money, and our businesses are no longer limited by physical boundaries. We can market anywhere in the world with ease.

I was recently in Ireland and found a boutique that I loved. Will they ship abroad? Yes. Are they on Facebook so that I am alerted to new products, and can I easily order their products through online ordering? Yes. Excellent—I now have a gift resource from across the pond, and it is not a big deal for me to shop there. That business in Ireland just went global!

Technology affords businesses the ability to more easily target customers and relay online messages that are more directed, which increases market share at a quicker pace.

How about the level of customer engagement we can all now enjoy thanks to the Internet and social networks? In my introduction I cited the top five reasons businesses fail. Number five was the inability to effectively engage with your target audience in order to understand their needs as they change and expand. Thanks to technology we now can obtain almost instant feedback.

Gathering immediate intelligence from your customers via social media channels allows for a quicker response to your customers' forever-changing needs. Responding to your customers quickly increases customer satisfaction and sales, and safeguards that your business will be an ongoing success.

Social media also provides an easy path to keep an eye on competitors and track changes in our target market. The ability to proactively respond to changes in the market caused by the innovation of our competition is critical.

Technology has removed the entry barrier to business ownership and allowed for an easier path to provide products and services on a global basis. It saves time and money, providing a road to growth and attaining VICTORY in your business.

The VICTORY Take-Away

Creating and implementing the strategies and tactics in each pillar of your business will bring your future vision into the present.

Remember the strategy of each pillar is what you want to accomplish. They are the goals of your blueprint. The tactics are the specific action steps you will take to accomplish the goals. I recommend utilizing the ancillary workbook to this book to create a written blueprint to build your business.

The seven pillars of a successful business are: operations, marketing, sales, customer service, finance, human resources and technology.

In this chapter, we reviewed each pillar and the creation of a strategy and supporting tactics to optimize results within each segment.

We began the chapter by reviewing operations and understanding the importance of developing an operational plan to ensure the business is operating at optimum efficiency.

The second pillar discussed marketing and recognizing its function as the driver of profits. We drilled into the process of developing a marketing strategy and presented the various traditional and digital channels to distribute your message.

At the core of your marketing strategy is your brand. Branding expert Joy Murphy revealed six keys to developing your brand to assure that your audience stays connected with your business. The marketing process provides the fuel for the sales process to create profits.

In the third section, we uncovered the sales process that produces results in this new technical era. We detailed how to have an insightful conversation and engage with customers and sell based on value, resulting in elevated conversion rates and higher profits.

In addition, Kurt Shaver, a LinkedIn Sales Solution Channel Partner, gave his expert advice on how to leverage LinkedIn as a sales tool to drive business.

Repeat sales are a result of continuously delivering exceptional service to our customers, and renowned customer service expert Shep Hyken presented tips to ensure delivering the highest customer service that creates customer loyalty and referrals.

The fifth pillar highlighted the benefits of understanding financial statements and underscored their pivotal role in making key management decisions that will fuel the success of your business.

The sixth pillar focused on creating a team to support your business. This section unlocked the keys as to how to source expertise and support for your business. From employees to independent contractors, scaling a business is not a job for one person.

The seventh pillar explored the benefits of integrating the use of technology into your business. Technology is the central reason as to why we can develop amazing, profitable businesses easier and more inexpensively now than ever before. It has granted us amazing connections and has expanded our reach worldwide.

Take Action

Operations

- Answer the questions In this chapter, regarding how your business will operate, produce and deliver your product or service, and develop an operations plan.
- Institute a system of periodic review of operations and create a plan to strengthen any weaknesses identified. Reviewing your operations will encourage you to remain agile in business as you respond to changes.

Marketing

- Identify your marketing objectives, develop a supporting marketing strategy and supporting tactics, and create a marketing calendar.
- Create a marketing message that will resonate with your target audience, and choose and implement a matrix of traditional and digital marketing channels to deliver your message.

Sales

- Create a very detailed ideal customer profile. Save time and increase conversions by qualifying each lead based upon the parameter of your ideal customer.
- Cultivate your customer by engaging in a consultative style of communication. Understand what the real value of your product or service is to each prospect and guide your customer through the decision-making process by articulating the solution you provide in the language of what they most value. Review how

effective you are in utilizing LinkedIn as a sales tool and institute the necessary changes as per Kurt Shaver's advice to effectively leverage this tool.

Customer Service

- Is your business creating an amazing experience for your customers? Assess how your customers rate your product and service. Take a survey, engage via social media or ask for their thoughts directly. The good, the bad, the ugly—find out how you rank in your customers' eyes. Identify any weaknesses in your customer service that are prohibiting your business from enjoying repeat business and shore up those weaknesses.
- Create a system to generate referrals. Follow up post-sale, ask for referrals and always express your gratitude.

Finance

- Understand how to read a financial statement and translate the information to provide guidance on management decisions. Commit to reviewing your financials monthly. Enlist the help of your CPA, if needed.
- Create a budget and establish a monthly review of the financial statements and comparison to the budget. Review all internal controls to ensure appropriate separation of duties.

Human Resources

- Assess if hiring new team members is necessary to grow your business and what specific areas of expertise you need to support your business.
- Hire according to the guidelines provided or source talent through non-traditional avenues, such as virtual assistants, internships, independent contractors, etc.

Technology

- Assess where efficiencies can be created in your business through the use of technology and activate the technology.
- Establish a specific strategy and an action plan to extend the boundaries of your business through the use of technology.

Chapter 4. Take Action and Be the Leader in Your Success

A RACE AGAINST THE CLOCK. As we get older, the clock seems to speed up, especially if you are actually racing against the clock. I have spent most of my life racing. Swim, bike, run.

Truth be told, I was a runner for years and entered the world of triathlons in my forties as a means to protect my knees from the incessant pounding of just running. But in a "tri," the racer is timed at every interval. Each section of the race is timed as you step on and off the individual timing mats. Mat swim, mat transition, mat bike, mat transition, mat run, mat finish. That is a lot of clock!

As I get older, the clock speeds up and, seemingly, my performance somehow deteriorates. In a race, they ease the blow of aging by segmenting the race by age groups, allowing you to evaluate your performance amongst your peers, as dictated by age. Next year, I will embrace turning fifty and the benefit of being the youngest in my 50-59 wave of competitors.

So, how do I hedge my bet each year as I ready for a new racing season? I am the leader in my world of success. I set goals, take continuous action and spend my time efficiently to ensure that I achieve each goal.

It is proven that when performance is measured, performance is increased—so I will continue to race against the clock and measure for as long as I can!

An overarching goal of every race, beyond beating the clock, is to not bonk! Bonking is when the body stops mid-race. Literally, your body and mind collapse. There are many theories as to why this happens: overtraining, lack of or inappropriate fuel level, dehydration.

It doesn't matter what the cause is. If it happens, the race is over. An athlete will do everything possible to avoid bonking by setting very specific training goals. Athletes create a plan for every pillar: body, mind and spirit.

With incessant determination, they will adhere to the plan until they achieve success. It is said that athletes are natural-born leaders and masters of their success. I don't believe this is innate and dictated by your DNA, but that leadership is a skill and can be developed.

Running a small business, just like any tri, is also a race against the clock as we compete to absorb market share and create keen strategies to avoid bonking in our climb to success.

Unfortunately, there are no allowances made for age or weaknesses of any kind. The antidote to failure? Becoming a leader, setting goals and taking consistent action in pursuit of your goals.

In this chapter, we will uncover the importance of being the leader of your life and practicing the core disciplines of a leader. We'll run through the process of creating specific, achievable goals with supporting strategies and tactics.

The Leverage It, Crutch It, Delegate It Time Management System™ will be revealed to guide you to be the master of your time and function at the highest productivity level.

Why Are Athletes Typically Strong Leaders?

Athletes have a make-up that allows them to push the envelope just a bit further than most, and these four qualities set them apart:

1. **Strategist** – Creating a strategy and a supporting plan to achieve is natural. Athletes are adept at creating goals and training plans that will drive achievement. Assessing risk, making decisions in response, planning, executing and measuring results is part of their everyday functionality.

2. **Focused** – Striving to be medal-worthy requires extreme focus. The ability to focus and keep the eyes on the prize is what drives athletes to win. They have a clear vision of what success looks like to them, and their ability to refocus their vision by remaining agile in responding to changes allows them to succeed when they come upon an obstacle.

3. **Team Players** – Athletes understand, whether they participate in an individual sport or are part of a team,

that success is in fact a team sport and is dependent
upon the contribution of many. Just like the
importance of cross-training, success is comprised of
the integration of many skills. These leaders are great
at mobilizing all of the support they need to realize
their success.

4. **Determination** – Athletes are determined. Working
   through challenges to peel off time, become stronger
   and realize their true potential is as natural as
   breathing. They understand the "ten thousand hour
   rule" to master a skill, and they don't mind putting in
   sweat equity to produce results. (The rule is that it
   takes 10,000 hours to become really proficient in a
   skill.)

Leadership is what sets the stellar platinum-medal businesses
apart from the mediocre businesses. But every business can be
stellar. Leadership is not only for the genetically gifted—it is a
right of birth. These attributes can be developed, bringing your
business to a higher level.

Why do many entrepreneurs fail? Because they set out with a
BHAG (Big Hairy Audacious Goal), but are not great leaders
and don't create supporting strategies and a heavyweight plan
of action to support achieving the darn hairy goal.

The small business owner has huge ambitions, limited time
and, most often, limited financial resources. Without having

clearly defined and supported goals, the hairy goal becomes the seemingly unattainable hairy monster.

Creating very specific goals, with supporting strategies and tactics, and instituting a stellar time management program will contribute a great deal towards achieving your vision of a successful business.

> *"Goals in writing are dreams with deadlines."*
>
> ~ Brian Tracy

Set a goal, write it down and give it a deadline. Period. This is the only way to move a business forward. Activate all employees and team members in the goal-setting process, as this will incite engagement and propel production levels and individual success.

We have all partaken in setting a goal on a whim, with no strategy to support reaching the goal. Who hasn't made a New Year's resolution at the stroke of midnight on January 1, only to suffer the failure and giving up phase by January 15? Or we set goals in each pillar of our business, but don't take the time to adequately plan and prepare to ensure achievement. Goals are your letter of intent to yourself and all the stakeholders in your business.

In order to realize your goals, the VICTORY goal achievement formula (a subset of the VICTORY process of establishing a business) is a very simple process that will ensure success:

Step 1 – Set the vision.
The vision is a clear statement of intent as to what will be achieved (with the thought that unlimited resources are

available). The vision is the promise to yourself and your stakeholders, and will keep you and your team motivated.

The vision must be detailed and clear, but also communicated in a fashion so that all within your organization understand why the vision is relevant.

From the vision, individual goals are created to support it. An example of a vision is: *"My business easily produces $500,000 net income each quarter."*

In order to bring your future vision into reality today, it's important to act as if it has already happened. We have all heard the term, "Fake it until you make it."

I love this saying, as the very act of pretending the future is already here is powerful. It will give confidence to team members to do things they wouldn't necessarily have the guts to do, and this provides the fuel needed to bring that future into the present.

Don't just envision the goals, *feel* the goals so that the emotion of already achieving is impactful and drives new behavior.

Your umbrella vision of what your business will achieve has many sub-visions and supporting goals. Successful business leaders create goals for all seven pillars of their business and for their own personal development. Goals keep us learning and striving towards achievement.

Step 2 – Identify the gap.

For each area of your business, assess where you are today in comparison to the stated goal. This is the gap. Be very detailed performing this analysis.

For example, if the goal is to increase gross profit margin in support of the vision of higher net income, ask the following:

- What are your actual sales numbers today?
- How many dollars does this constitute, per sale?
- How many clients or customers do you have today?
- What are the margins on the sales of your product or service?
- What are the costs of your goods sold?
- What is the quality of your customers?
- What percent of sales is from repeat customers or new customers?

With your analyses, identify the true gaps:

- Where is there room for improvement?
- Do you need more customers?
- Do you need higher quality customers?
- Is your pricing structure correct?
- Can you increase margins to increase sales?
- Is there a customer retention issue?

It is impossible to create a blueprint to achieve your goals if you don't know exactly what it is you need to achieve. Again, we need measurements.

If the goal is to increase sales by 30% by the end of the second quarter, you need to ask: What are my sales today? What exactly is the dollar amount that I need to increase my sales by?

Step 3 – Create strategies and tactics to support your goal.

Strategy is the planning process of how the goal will be achieved. *Tactics* are the actions employed to carry out the strategy.

Before we get into creating strategies and tactics, it is important to understand and embrace the fact that where your business is today is because you, the leader—and only you—created the reality.

It is important to take full responsibility for the successes as well as the failures in your business. The strategies and tactics employed to move towards attainment of your goals are yours to create, and only you are responsible for their creation and execution. No excuses—success or failure is all YOU!

And don't be afraid of failure. If, in the review stage, the result is that a particular strategy or action step didn't produce the results needed to meet the goal, simply revise. But don't let fear or lack of planning hold you back.

For each goal, ask the following questions:

1. What resources are needed to achieve the goal?

   For example, based on the identification of the gaps, does the organization have the production capacity to increase sales? Where will new customers come from?

2. What additional talents are needed or additional training required in my organization in order to meet the goal?

   For example, is additional sales training needed for the team in order to increase sales?

3. Who can assist in achieving the goal?

   For example, do we need new suppliers that can provide the same quality or better product or supplies for production at a less expensive cost to help increase margins? Or do we need additional high-priced items in the product line to drive sales?

4. Why is this goal necessary to bring our future vision into the present?

   For example, achieving higher margins will have a more direct and quicker impact on increasing net income than other strategies.

The answers to the above questions will help to formulate the strategy to accomplish the goal and will guide the creation of the action steps, or tactics, necessary to achieve the goal. The questions will also force an assessment as to how difficult the goal is in relation to the present skill levels available.

As an example, the strategy to support a goal of increasing gross profit margin by 10% becomes:

Gross profit margin will be increased by:

- Increasing the dollar amount per sale by offering a higher price point product.
- Reviewing and assessing current price points on the product line.
- Identifying additional resources to provide product at a lower cost, decreasing cost of sales.

Executing specific tactics then supports the strategies.

Such as:

The following action steps will increase gross profit:

- Identify products that integrate with the current product line and are in demand by customers at a higher price point.
- Integrate new products into the current product line.
- Review all costs, variable and fixed, that are associated with the current product line and assess appropriateness of price level relative to costs and within the current market.
- Review and identify additional suppliers that may provide supplies and materials at a lower cost point.

These are just a few samples of tactics that support the strategies identified to support the goal. There will be many tactics or actions steps to support each strategy.

Frequently, a client will not want to take the time to do the proper planning, and I am often asked "How do I know when I have planned enough?"

You will have created a proper amount of strategy and tactics when you have written it out and someone else other than yourself can carry out the plan to achieve the goal.

Create very clear benchmarks of success for all strategies and tactics. What will indicate achievement as the strategies are implemented? What numbers, measurement and metrics will provide an indicator that you are moving forward positively?

It is important to enjoy the journey as you and your team move towards achieving the goals, so always celebrate each benchmark of success along the way.

Step 4 – Become the master of your time, and take action towards achieving your goals.

Time is our most precious resource and, unfortunately, our most limited resource available. If you feel that you are always fighting against the clock, trust me, it doesn't have to be that way. When you make that transition into entrepreneurship from a more structured environment, figuring out how to best utilize your time can be a huge challenge.

The most frequent excuse I hear from clients struggling to achieve their goals is their perceived lack of time. I understand, we are all stretched to the hilt and struggling to balance our business, our personal life, commitments to our community, etc. I get it.

Why do some people seem to manage their time easier than others? How do we become the masters of our time? Simply by creating systems that save time and knowing how to make every minute count.

Small business owners love to micromanage their businesses, but the reality is there is not enough time to be a micro-manager.

By taking action consistently you will move forward. Often I see people become paralyzed by the massive plan of strategies and tactics. Stay out of that overwhelming feeling by breaking down your steps into bite-size chunks.

It is easy to become distracted by the demands of an unknown project that is dropped on your lap by a client, or by the demands of your personal life. As a small business owner, the challenge to stay focused while balancing the various pillars of the business—as well as your personal life—is daunting.

Each day, I recommend mapping out your day and creating a chunk of must-dos and creating a time within your day that you will focus on completing those tasks. With persistence you will make progress.

Elevate your productivity and performance by implementing these time management tips.

Leverage It, Crutch It, Delegate It
Time Management System

Unfortunately, we are taught at a very young age to focus on our weaknesses in order to improve the skills that seem to be lacking. So instead of celebrating and leveraging our strengths, we spend our time focused on areas that are difficult and lacking. And we end up wasting our time.

It is true that owning a small business requires us to be adept in many broad functions of running a business—however, the majority of our time should be spent focused in areas of our strengths. These areas tend to be our income-producing areas and where we are most effective in driving profits for our business.

To become the master of your time, it's important to **leverage** your areas of strength, and focus the majority of time on those activities. These are the areas of expertise that you are most comfortable in or have a specific talent for and, therefore, these are the tasks you are most efficient performing.

The tasks that you don't have specific knowledge to perform well but your involvement is necessary for, need a **crutch**. For example, it is important that your finances be done correctly and that you understand your financial statement so that you may make sound business decisions, but you are not an accountant. Hire a CPA to perform the actual finance work, and utilize the CPA to guide you to understand the meaning of your financial statements. Your CPA becomes your financial crutch.

The activities that are a must, but that you do not possess the expertise for (or are below your ultimate skill level), should be **delegated**. For example, you need to create marketing collateral to promote your business, but you are not a graphic designer. This clearly needs to be a delegated task. Or if you have activities that you are performing that are not the core of your expertise and not income-producing, those duties need to be delegated.

Most frequently, new business owners are reluctant to hire anyone because they are cash poor. However, by not delegating tasks that are not driving cash flow, relieving you to the core moneymaking activities, you are cutting off your nose to spite your face. When do you know it is time to crutch or delegate a task? When less than 80% of your time is spent on income-producing activities.

To be most efficient and increase productivity that hits the bottom line, make a list of every duty that is a function of the business and decide if each activity is to be leveraged, crutched or delegated.

Identify resources that can be utilized as a crutch and sources that can accept delegated duties that are outside of your expertise. Focus your energy and expertise only upon activities that leverage your unique talents and produce high-level results.

Time is money, so here are a few top timesaving tips:

1. Understand your priorities and what activities will create the greatest success in reaching the goals of your business. It is the old 80/20 rule. 80% of your sales are derived from 20% of your customers. The same goes for your time. 20% of what your business does will produce 80% of the positive results, so be sure your time is focused upon the 20% that is producing 80% of the results.

2. Every evening, create a written plan of action that supports movement towards your goals, and stick to your plan. Create a top five "must do's" list, and don't leave your office until those five are done. Begin your day attacking the top five.

3. Focus. Stop trying to poorly multitask. Snuff out the distractions and you may begin to realize the advantages of hyper-focus. Block your days by tasks. Set up time to do all of your phone calls at once, your administration in one block, your creative work in another block, etc. Working on like tasks blocked together creates efficiencies. Be aware of your

individual energy level and when your performance is at its best for certain tasks. Set designated times to check email, voicemail and social media feeds. Literally turn off your devices and emails so as not to be tempted during focus periods.

4. Utilize the Swiss cheese approach, which is to break large tasks into bite-size chunks and fill small, 5 - 10 minute gaps in the day with those activities. This is really helpful when moving between blocks of designated activities or for filling gaps of time when waiting for others.

5. Do not confuse activity for achievement. Slugging around in the weeds and not making sales call is not an effective use of time. Be mindful of where you spend your time and what is truly moving you towards your goals. Limit interruptions from phone calls and employees by not accepting unplanned conversations during designated periods of productive work.

6. Get real and don't go for perfection. If you are a perfectionist and wasting loads of time being stuck in the mud waiting for the perfect time to launch, the reality is you may never launch. Recognize that any project will most likely not ever be exact, so don't waste time endlessly perfecting a project. Be brave and launch the project, and then review, revise and re-do as needed. Need guidance on being a perfectionist?

Check out the book *Too Perfect: When Being in Control Gets Out of Control* by Allan E. Mallinger, M.D. and Jeannette DeWyze. (Find it online at chrisvanderzyden.com/TooPerfect.)

7. Honor the "touch it once" rule. Open the mail, touch it once and move it forward and off your desk. Purge your inbox, email and desk to keep the bottomless paper pit to a minimum. Create email templates for repeated types of emails or notices.

8. Take advantage of technology to save time. Automate as much as possible in your business, from lead generation to conversion. Utilize apps, such as Google, to simplify and streamline tasks and facilitate collaboration with partners. Save travel time by utilizing video services, such as Skype or GoToMeeting, to connect with customers, employees or partners. Utilize your customer relationship management (CRM) tool as much as possible.

    Here are a few of my favorite tech aids:
    - **Nimble** – a terrific social media CRM system
    - **SalesForce** – used to be for large companies but not anymore—check out their Enterprise Package for Small to Midsize Businesses
    - **LogMeIn** – allows you to connect to your computer remotely (I love this for when I am traveling or working in a remote location.)

- **Jott Assistant** – if you are on the move and can't write at the moment, this tool allows you to call a number, speak your thoughts, and they transcribe and send the note to your email. Brilliant!

- **Evernote** – a digital filing system that is searchable

9. Take breaks and increase your performance. Yes, take time to regroup and recharge and you will find yourself more productive. During your day, schedule time to walk away from your work, allowing you downtime to refocus. Studies have shown that taking even a ten-minute break increases focus and production level. How about vacations? I know the feeling of being an entrepreneur and not being able to truly leave the office. It took me years to figure that one out. A few ideas. Hire a project manager to oversee the business while you are gone. Forge a relationship with another business in your area of expertise and watch over each other's businesses while taking breaks. Start a month in advance and work with every client to be sure your clients' needs are taken care of, and schedule the workload around your holiday.

10. If you are easily distracted or tend to go over the time allotted for a particular task, utilize a time app, such as 30/30, to keep you moving along in your day.

Step 5 – Make a plan for your obstacles.

Not all obstacles are easily identifiable. However, hedge your bets by identifying known weaknesses. Make a list of what you can conceive as an obstruction that will keep you from taking the action necessary to move forward in reaching your goals.

For example, I frequently hear, "I don't like to make follow-up calls, so I tend to call the customers that I know really well, have a chat and then stop there."

They never follow-up with the leads that truly need to be converted into paying customers. Why? They are afraid the lead will say "no."

Great! Acknowledge the fear. By understanding the roadblocks that keep you from taking action, you can create a plan to release the blocks. Make a list of every potential obstacle, and create a strategy to overcome each block.

In this example, the sales person might list all of the follow-up calls that need to be made and make the most difficult calls first, saving the fun, feel-good follow-up calls until last as a reward.

By understanding your weaknesses and being clever in creating action steps to overcome obstructions, your success rate will skyrocket.

Step 6 – Consistently review your progress.

Reviewing the benchmarks of success on a daily basis provides the opportunity to acknowledge how well you are progressing towards your goals. It will highlight the deficiencies that are slowing you down and will allow you to make the necessary adjustments and course corrections to the action plan.

Look for quantitative indicators, such as dollars, quantity of production and time. Be agile in considering new approaches and techniques. There may be a way to achieve your goal faster and more economically, so be willing to pivot and go another route if that makes sense.

Also, keep in mind the key motivators that drive you. The core value assessment performed in the first chapter will provide guidance to understand what intrinsic motivators inspire you to engage in business. Motivation is sustained when goals are tied to intrinsic values rather than extrinsic desires, such as possessions or money. Emotional motivators will provide the stamina necessary to overcome any obstacle.

A strategy to ensure that motivation is kept at an optimal level is to create a reward for each goal met. Yes, intrinsic motivators are chief, but it is fine to specify a "treat" to reward your success. Something as simple as a walk in the woods can be a reward for extended, focused attention on a project.

Hang with the Yeasayers

Having trouble reaching your goals? Be sure to hang out with the yeasayers and avoid the obstructionists. Your influencers have tremendous impact on your success, so be sure to have a positive circle of influence, with quality people who are supportive of your goals.

Communicate your goals to your support team. It is amazing how focused we become in achieving our goals when we have announced our intent to the world!

Create an accountability system. This can be as simple as having a buddy you check in with to compare progress, or it can be a more formalized group, such as a mastermind group.

Hire a coach, consultant or a guide. Whatever you do, be sure that you have the proper support to help you achieve your goals within the time frame that you specify.

We'll discuss motivation more in depth in the last chapter. However, if you find yourself struggling to continue to take action, look back at how far you have come in reaching your goal and this will spur you on to keep moving forward.

Often, I will ask a client who is having a particularly tough time to write and review all of their past successes. This will serve as a reminder of your capabilities and will push you forward.

The VICTORY Take-Away

To continue to productively work toward VICTORY in your business, you must become the leader of your success, set goals, create specific action steps towards achievement, and be the master of your time.

It requires a daily commitment to maintain a high productivity level. Make a conscious decision and choose to be self-disciplined to take action on a daily basis—you will meet your goals and ultimately increase your profits.

Take Action

- Create clear personal and professional goals that will support your vision.
- Develop the strategies and tactics to achieve your goals—create a detailed plan to the extent that someone else may execute it in your absence.
- Create a daily time management plan, and adhere to reviewing your progress daily.

Chapter 5. Converting Obstacles Into Opportunities

As I MENTIONED, SWITCHING TO triathlons was a strategy to save my knees from years of running, but there was one tiny, little issue—I have always been scared of swimming in open water.

When I was very young, I was swimming in the ocean and my Dad suddenly scooped me out of the water because a stingray had surprisingly appeared. The lifeguard pulled the stingray out of the water for all of us at the beach to see.

Well, that made an amazing impact on me, and I decided right then and there I was not going to ever put myself in a position where a stingray, or any fish for that matter, could swim with me. Fear.

I once tried to overcome the fear by swimming at Stingray City in the Grand Cayman Islands, but that didn't really turn out well. I couldn't quite get myself to keep my snorkeling face in the water!

But I really wanted to transition into tris because I believed that cross-training would allow me to be more physically active for a longer period in my life. So I acknowledged the fear for what it was and created a few strategies to help me overcome the obstacle.

Number one, I always wear a wetsuit so that I can't feel the kelp or anything else that may appear.

Number two, I always swim with a buddy just in case some scary foreign object appears, and then at least I will have someone with me.

Number three, I recognize that I am out of my comfort zone; I embrace the fear for what it is; and I choose to love the water.

Truth? I'm still not totally comfortable in the water, but my fear does not keep me from doing what I love to do. I race, enjoy and never think about what is in the water or at the bottom of the lake or ocean!

Obstacles in life and in business are plentiful, and you will continuously encounter challenges as you grow. Fortunately, there are many strategies and tools that can be utilized to keep you moving along your path of success.

A wetsuit was my shield of armor against my fear, but there are many different types of obstacles and a corresponding solution for every obstacle.

Obstacles are merely opportunities in disguise. The quicker a challenge is viewed as an opportunity, the faster a resolution is identified and movement is made through the gateway to growth.

Too many entrepreneurs get stuck, become overwhelmed and allow the interference to block them from success. Unfortunately, small businesses typically don't plan for the impending obstacles; much less create a plan to overcome them.

Of course, it is much more comfortable to live in the land of "all is well," but that is not reality, and change is inevitable. If you are to succeed and achieve your goals, planning for the obstacles as much as you can will go a long way towards achieving success in your business.

In this chapter, we will identify external and internal obstacles that threaten to derail you from achieving success. Then we are going to present a few tools to help guide you to overcome the challenges and keep your motivation running high.

External Obstacles

Let's explore the various obstacles that may threaten your business. External obstacles are those created by factors we have no control over, such as market competition, political or legal changes, or changing technology.

Competition within your industry can be a positive if you innovate and prepare. By responding to change, your business will rise to new levels, creating more profits and more success.

Changing laws can cause disruption in the economy, creating new markets to be filled. Consider Obamacare. The new healthcare law tripped up the healthcare industry, but created more opportunity for those who were positioned to respond.

Technology is forever changing, and this is an obstacle that has proven to create enormous benefits. Just think about how we can engage with our customers through the Internet, creating better customer service and an ease in identifying customers' changing needs.

All of these examples are obstacles that can trip up a business, unless embraced as an opportunity and reacted to positively.

Remember the SWOT analysis you did in chapter one? Strengths, weaknesses, opportunities and threats? That exercise of identifying possible opportunities and threats is your window to future external obstacles.

A SWOT analysis is not a one-time gig that you do when you are preparing to launch a business. This is a tool to keep your business growing and should be performed on a regular basis.

Keep ahead of changes and create a plan within your organization to counteract obstacles. Some outside threats can include increased competition, economic downturns, or a supplier shift. The outside threats are out of your control; however, by being aware of impending changes, it allows for the creation of contingency plans to counteract the obstacle and create opportunities.

How do you stay ahead of the curve? Be engaged, read the news, read your industry trade magazines, interact with your colleagues and your competition. Take the information in, be insightful as to how the changes will ultimately impact your business, and create a strategy to positively react.

There are many kinds of obstacles that you will encounter in running your business, from customer relations, to employees, to business development…the list goes on.

Your success will largely be determined by how creative your solutions are and how you choose to react. Fortunately, how we choose to react is entirely at our discretion.

Employees will follow the leaders in an organization, so be sure all of the team leaders respond positively—employees will then be inspired to be more creative in resolving the challenges they come upon on a daily basis.

A common obstacle for small business is landing the big client. Sounds great, doesn't it? How can this possibly present a challenge? Well, preparing for reeling in the big fish requires a strategy as to how you will service the big fish. Will you need more employees? How will you ensure that your big fish doesn't place you in an "all eggs in one basket" scenario? While you are focused on the big, moneymaking client, how will you continue to market to ensure you don't have a feast or famine situation once the big fish swims out to a different sea?

Get my drift? Almost all successes come with an obstacle, and your ability to create sustained success will be determined by how well you prepare for and respond to the challenges.

Another common obstacle, as discussed previously in chapter three, is the current hyper-competitive sales environment. Most businesses today are faced with price wars and eroding profit margins, which presents a real obstacle in capturing your target.

Here are a few tips to overcome price wars:

1. **Tighten up your targets.** Identify organizations that are agile in their decision-making process and have the potential to make a change. These prospects are open to new solutions, have the ability to quickly change direction and are not solely focused on price. Identify these organizations by researching their purchasing vendor selection criteria. Do they entertain new vendors? Do they elicit bid requests?

   A company that has a strict purchasing protocol and is inflexible will be more price-sensitive and less likely to entertain new ideas as solutions to their challenges.

2. **Time your outreach to industry-wide changes.** Take action and engage your customers prior to the time they need your product or service.

   Be aware of changes within your target market's industry and external pressures, such as new government regulations, that will create a need. Identifying unrecognized needs prior to your customer creates opportunity for you to contact your prospect and have a consultative-style conversation that evokes trust. When it is time for your customer to react to the change, you are well positioned, as you have already had a discussion and provided compelling reasons to choose your product or service as the solution.

3. **Be the leader and the expert.** Guide your client through the decision process and present why your company's core strengths and service or product will benefit them. By approaching your potential customer as a consultant-advisor and relaying the fact that your expertise will greatly benefit them, you will build trust—and trust is the cornerstone to converting a prospect into a loyal customer.

Be creative and let your leadership shine through!

Internal Obstacles

Then there are the hold-us-down, internal obstacles that bind us to inaction—those bad boys that really try to stop us from achieving our goals. They are mostly rooted in fears, like my fear of unexpected stingrays in water. Fear. Yes, False Evidence Appearing Real.

I don't believe we can overcome our fears, but do believe we can learn to manage our fears so they don't impede our progress.

The first step to harnessing our internal obstacles is to identify what the obstacles are. Be honest with yourself and assess what is truly holding you back and keeping you stuck:

- Are you afraid of success?
- Are you afraid of failure?

- Are you afraid of money—the lack of, or having too much and then the fear that somehow you will lose it!
- Are you afraid to hire an employee because you don't trust that you will find and hire the right team member?
- Are you afraid to go out and market your business?
- Are you afraid a potential customer will say no?

Fear is a powerful hindrance to progress. Fear anchors us from obtaining our goals. Whether we are striving to move our business to a new level, lose weight or live an authentic life, fear is a force that creates resistance to change that can appear to be insurmountable.

When working with clients, I frequently ask them to tell me what exactly they feel they need to do—something that they are not currently doing—which will make them more successful. A very simple question; and frequently, they will tell me in a split second what they are not doing.

It will forever amaze me that we understand our fears so well, yet the grip remains and is able to stop us dead in our tracks. Typically, it isn't all that simple, and peeling back layers to identify the true underlying fear that keeps us from moving forward is necessary. For instance, if we have a fear of calling on a new customer, it isn't just the fear of meeting someone new, but the fear of possibly hearing "no."

And it really isn't hearing the word "no"—the fear is what does the "no" represent? Many times there is one action that can be taken that will make all of the difference in the world to the success of a business.

Once we have identified the root of the fear, we can then create a strategy to be implemented to move forward.

Here are three steps to help manage your fear and keep you in a mode of action:

1. **Identify your fear** – Fear lets you know that you are going to make a change and that you may not understand the result. The unknown is scary to most people. Identify exactly what the fear is. Pay attention to your internal dialogue as to why you can't do something to uncover the core of your fear.

   When I hear clients say, "I'm afraid," that is when I really start cheering, as I know they are in the process of identifying their fear and are on their way to taking action. The first step towards success is identify the fear, whatever it is, that keeps you in a stagnate position.

2. **Embrace your fear –** Ask yourself, "What is the worst possible outcome?" Ninety percent of what we worry about never happens. So worrying about failure or the result of your success is senseless and a waste of time. If the worst outcome you imagine does indeed happen, then your worrying about that scenario affords you the fearful experience not once but twice—once with worry and a second time when it actually happens! Don't waste time worrying about the ugly scenario that your mind has conjured up and is not a reality.

I also don't believe we can overcome our fears. We can only master the action necessary to work through our fears in order to keep us moving forward. Embrace your fears, create a rock solid strategy to work through them, and bravely implement your strategy.

3. **Choose action** – Understand that fear can be useful. Fear will make you pause to really think through your strategy. Being fearless can be detrimental and downright scary. Fearlessness can cause you to move forward when you should not, so utilize the fear to get clear on your strategy, and then jump into the change.

In the end, the choice to accept the risk, take action and live life to the highest potential is all up to you. Everyone has the power to choose to overcome fear, and take action or not.

Tools to Help You Overcome Fear

I have observed many entrepreneurs and solopreneurs who seem to be perfectly positioned for success. They have done everything seemingly right. They have created a great business model, identified their value proposition and marketed accordingly. They have their systems and processes in place, yet they falter, and I am amazed. I see a huge amount of potential for success, yet there is some piece of the puzzle that isn't fitting—some interference that keeps them from taking the action that will produce the result.

As a business consultant, and having had my own experiences of not being able to break through an obstacle, I started to research alternative approaches. I have watched time and time again people who have a great blueprint for success, but a barrier keeps them from achieving. Then I started to take note of the conversations or excuses, and many times I realized it was rooted in fear or some other limiting belief.

In my quest to uncover alternative solutions to overcoming fears—other than the mantra, "Just do it"—I was introduced to tapping by Jack Canfield. I was in Bali with Jack on a business retreat and he introduced me to Tapping, or Emotional Freedom Technique (EFT), and encouraged me to integrate the approach into my business consulting practice.

Tapping is sometimes referred to as "emotional acupuncture," having evolved from the ancient Chinese medicine of acupuncture. The technique involves tapping on "energy meridians" in an effort to open the gateway to emotional freedom.

We all hold conscious and unconscious beliefs that can keep us from taking the action that will be effective towards driving us to our success. Tapping on the meridians interrupts the fear response in the brain.

EFT is a process of tapping on pressure points while repeating key phrases out loud. This action sends deactivating signals to the fear center of the brain, which then interrupt the feeling of fear.

Tapping is a system of transforming limiting beliefs and creating new positive and empowering beliefs.

At the time I had no idea what EFT was. Jack led me through the process with amazing results. I didn't use my fear of water, but a more common fear that I speak a great deal about with my clients: lack of money. The fear of not having "enough" is deeply engrained in many people, and typically this fear is created by a childhood memory. Having been brought up in a middle-class family myself, money was presented as something that was difficult to come by, and this perception of lack of money created a fear.

So, Jack and I tapped away…

The first question Jack asked me was to identify my level of fear was on a scale of 1 – 10. Easy, a 10. We went through the process:

Step 1: Take note of the level of distress you feel on a scale of 1 - 10. This is called the Subjective Units of Distress, or SUDS, level. Think of this like when you go to the doctor for physical pain and they ask you to assess your pain on a scale of 1 - 10. This is the same, but for EFT assess your emotional pain. To what degree is your fear inhibiting your life?

Step 2: Create a specific "set-up phrase," such as "*Even though I am afraid that I will not make enough money, I totally and completely love and accept myself.*" Repeat your set-up phrase while tapping on the karate chop point (the soft part of the non-dominant hand below the pinky finger) several times.

Step 3: Begin tapping at your meridian points while saying out loud a reminder phrase that verbalizes your fear so you acknowledge and feel the fear. This reminder phrase is your articulation of what the fear is. For example, it could be "*If I am not successful I will become a poor bag lady living in the streets*" or "*If I am not financially successful nobody will love me.*"

The meridian points are at the top of the head, at the eyebrow point (center between your eyebrows), outside of the eye (at the outside lower corner of the eye), under the eye, under the nose, the indentation above your chin, the collarbone, about four inches under the armpit and the karate chop (used for the set-up phrase). While tapping at each meridian say a reminder phrase as to what your fear is to draw up the negative emotion. It is important to feel the fear while tapping.

THE TAPPING POINTS

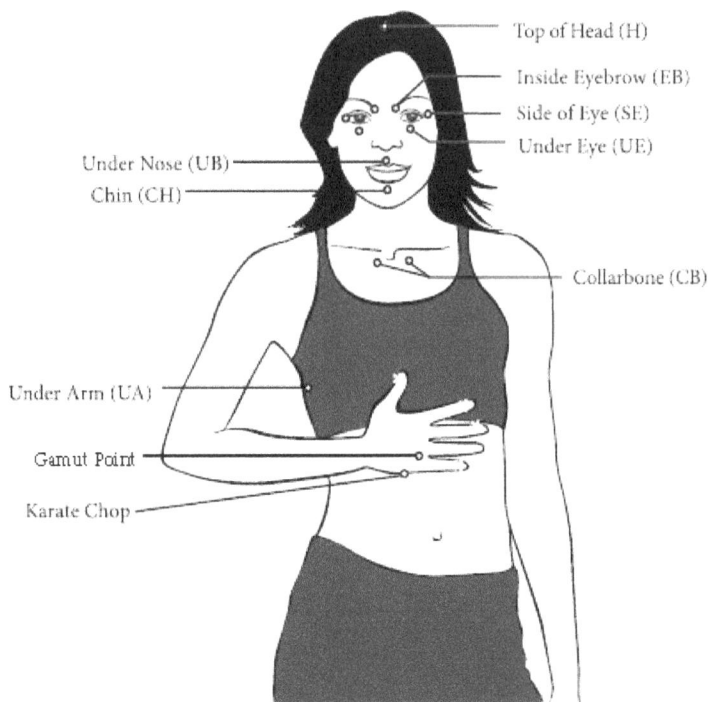

Top of Head (H)
Inside Eyebrow (EB)
Side of Eye (SE)
Under Eye (UE)
Under Nose (UB)
Chin (CH)
Collarbone (CB)
Under Arm (UA)
Gamut Point
Karate Chop

Top of head *(H)*	Inside Eyebrow *(EB)*
Side of Eye *(SE)*	Under Eye *(UE)*
Under Nose (UB)	Chin *(CH)*
Collarbone *(CB)*	Under Arm *(UA)*

HAND: Thumb, Index Finger, Middle Finger, Little Finger, Karate Chop/Side of hand.

While tapping the meridian points, say your reminder phrases:

TOP OF THE HEAD: I'm afraid I won't be financially successful.

EYEBROW: I'm afraid I will fail and my family will be hurt.

OUTSIDE OF THE EYE: I'm afraid my business won't succeed.

UNDER THE EYE: I'm afraid I will become a bag lady.

UNDER THE NOSE: If I fail it will be so embarrassing.

CHIN: I'm afraid I can't make money.

COLLARBONE: What will my family think if I don't make enough money?

UNDER THE ARM: I would be so ashamed if I failed.

Tap two rounds, acknowledging and feeling your fear.

Step 4: After the two rounds of tapping, ask yourself what your SUDS level is on a scale of 1 to 10. If your suds level is 3 or above, proceed to step 5.

Step 5: Repeat the set-up phrase tapping the karate chop point and doing two more rounds of the simple tapping using reminder phrases that alternate the negative emotions with a positive affirmation. A positive affirmation will serve to disconnect the fear and endorse the true reality.

For example:

SET-UP PHRASE: Even though I am afraid that I will not make enough money, I totally and completely love and accept myself.

NEGATIVE EMOTION: It will be so embarrassing if I fail and don't make enough money.

POSITIVE AFFIRMATION: I know my family will still love me if I don't make enough money.

NEGATIVE EMOTION: But if I fail it will hurt my family.

POSITIVE AFFIRMATION: I know that I am perfectly capable of generating the income I desire.

Step 6: Assess your SUDS level. You may experience a complete abatement of the feelings of fear or at least a reduced level of anxiety.

My experience with Jack was that at the end of the process I had no feeling of the financial fear that just moments ago dominated my thoughts. Jack remarked that it was funny watching me, as I began to look around for the feeling of fear, as if I had lost some object like my coffee cup! I can only describe the dissipation as the feeling of fear seemingly just draining out of me.

Sometimes the technique has immediate results, as it did with me, and sometimes it takes more sessions. There is much support and evidence of success with the technique. Since my experience in Bali, I have tried to recall the financial fear to no avail.

I also have a friend who used tapping to rid herself of the fear of flying. She reports that it worked beautifully, and not only did it get rid of the fear of flying; it rid her of the fear of turbulence too!

I can correlate many business failures to succumbing to fear. For example, in the case of fear of calling on a customer, I can give a client a script and we can role-play, but if the block is fear-based they won't present authentically. Will this inhibit the client's success level? Absolutely. Do our fears limit our profits? Yes.

EFT is a powerful technique that can deliver results, and very fast. So if you feel stuck or have experienced the same situational outcomes in the past and cannot figure out a way to overcome the block, I recommend you investigate this technique. Jack Canfield and Pamela Bruner wrote a great book that is a terrific resource, called *Tapping into Ultimate Success*. (Find it online at chrisvanderzyden.com/Tapping.)

Motivation

As you strive to grow your business and drive profits, what will keep you motivated as you encounter external and internal obstacles?

Motivation is the force that drives the action necessary to overcome our obstacles and succeed in achieving our goals. Maintaining motivation, and the level of your motivation, will determine your ability to persist in the face of challenges.

Just like there are externally and internally generated obstacles, there are external and internal motivators. The internal motivators will drive you further and faster.

As mentioned previously, external motivators are those that are extrinsic, such as a car or money. These motivators are fleeting and are not as powerful in driving you to keep going in the face of adversity like internal motivators will. Every car loses that new car smell pretty quickly!

Internal motivators speak to your core values and provide greater stamina in reaching your goals. Internal motivators are emotional in nature and respond to a sense of purpose. It's understanding why you are choosing to do what you are doing.

Internal motivation is derived from acting in alignment with your core values. For example, one of my core values is to teach and give back, so I am motivated to write this book by my desire to inform and make running a small business easier for the reader.

Internal motivators are derived from your inner self. To further understand in-depth what motivates you to achieve, I recommend participating in the Values Online Ranking process at valuesonline.net, which will guide you to align your actions with your values and result in a higher degree of purposeful action, helping you maintain your motivation in the face of any adversity presented.

Be clear on what your motivators are. Ask yourself "Why am I doing what I'm doing?" Uncover what motivates you internally after the vacations, the cars, etc. Write down your key motivators as a reminder to refer to when the road gets rocky and you need a boost to keep moving forward.

Strategies to keep your motivation running high:

1. Create a daily gratitude list of the progress you made towards reaching your goals.

2. Chart your progress and review it to reaffirm the progress you have already made. It is really hard to quit when you realize how far you have come.

3. Make a list of all of the obstacles you have overcome in the past. Past performance is a great indicator of future

performance, and this process will give you confidence in your ability to overcome.

4. Visualize your success several times a day. In your head, play out the desired result and the feelings that are attached to the positive outcome.

5. Acknowledge that you feel like quitting, and then institute your strategy to overcome that urge.

6. Keep reminders of "why" you are doing what you are doing everywhere—office, desk, car, mirror.

7. Be inspired. Tune in and talk to people who are already successful in the business you are in.

8. Be patient. Recognize that success takes time.

9. Don't stay in your comfort zone. With new experiences, our motivation is uplifted.

10. Get an accountability buddy. It is easier to stay motivated when there are two people striving to succeed and pulling each other forward.

Failure and Resilience

If you fail in overcoming an obstacle, your resilience will save you!

I had an advertising specialty company that had an epic crash and burn scenario. We had been working for a large entertainment company for several years when we landed the "big project." This project was going to be great, and we were ready to take it on with a plan for huge success. It was complicated and exceedingly time-sensitive, and huge marketing dollars were dependent on the success of this project. We were ready, and I was confident in my team members.

Well, our client's creative director and I had scheduled our vacation in tandem so that no time would be lost. Unfortunately, my vacation was in London, and I had committed to my family that I would not work for the six days we were there so I confidently left my laptop and blackberry behind.

Mother Nature was not on my side however, and I was trapped an additional nine days in London, as all planes were grounded due to the Icelandic volcano. No problem. I, like every other American committed to work, ran to the closest Apple store, bought myself a computer, had my assistant pull every file over to Mobile Me, and I continued to work seamlessly from London until we got a flight home.

I had chased that obstacle down and as our deadline approached felt confident in our success. The day before the launch, we were all doing the woohoo success dance. This was going to be great. My client was going to love this project when it was delivered to their office.

The next day we unfortunately received a call from our client with the report that the project had been improperly packed and destroyed in transit. And I mean destroyed. We had to pay to have it rebuilt. Was it our fault? Technically, no, we did not pack it for shipping, but I had chosen the fulfillment house and obviously didn't give enough direction to them.

Did I take a financial hit? You bet, and a big hit. Did I learn from that mistake? Quickly. Onward and upward.

Don't be afraid of failure. Our success is the culmination of all that we have learned when we have failed. Every step forward includes risk, and some risk is unforeseen. But those steps, even if deemed a failure in the end, are part of the road to success if you learn from the failure, adjust and move on quickly.

So fail huge. Take a risk and succeed or fail big—and I mean really big, huge, going-down-in-flames big. When I hear about big failures, I know that huge successes are on the way, so embrace your fear and go for it.

Many successful people have had huge failures prior to their success. We spoke about a few at the beginning of the book, but here are a few more:

- Oprah Winfrey was fired from one of her early jobs as a television reporter.
- Donald Trump was $1 billion in debt in the early 1990s.
- Babe Ruth ended up with the home run record, but he also had the record for the most strikeouts.
- Winston Churchill lost every election for public office, until he became prime minister.
- Jerry Seinfeld was booed off stage the first time he walked on a stage.
- Vincent Van Gogh only sold one painting during his lifetime, and that was to a friend.

Success is just a compilation of our failures. And every time you fail, you are closer to success.

Today, small businesses that have endured our disruptive economy have done so by proving they are nimble and able to positively react in the face of adversity. These companies have created opportunities out of obstacles.

There are, of course, examples of very successful companies that ultimately failed because of their inflexibility. One exceptionally colossal failure was **Eastman Kodak**.

This is a story about how deep-seated fear of failure and lack of agility can immobilize an organization and create a colossal failure.

George Eastman, the founder of Eastman Kodak Company, was a great entrepreneur whose ability to recognize and positively react to change created one of the greatest film companies of all time.

Mr. Eastman proactively responded to change in developing his company by moving from a dry-plate process to film, and then from black and white film to color. He proved himself to be agile in responding to change and, in the process, created great success.

In addition to his success as an entrepreneur, he was an enormously generous philanthropist. His love for music compelled him to endow the Eastman School of Music. He also established the schools of dentistry and medicine at the University of Rochester.

Unfortunately, he suffered from chronic pain in his later years and ended his life on March 14, 1932 by shooting himself in the heart and leaving a note behind which read, "To my friends: My work is done. Why wait?" Remarkable.

His legacy will forever live on. However, sadly, The Eastman Kodak company today struggles as a result of its inability to positively react to industry change.

In 1965, Steve Sasson, a Kodak engineer, invented the first digital camera. Management unfortunately refused to recognize and embrace the new technology as an opportunity for growth. Instead, they viewed the filmless camera as a threat to their existing core business—photo film and printing.

Kodak's complacency, lack of opportunity recognition (ironically created by their own engineer) and inability to effectively adapt to change were strong contributors to the deterioration of the company.

They failed because of their lack of agility and inability to deviate from their core business and respond to the technological advancement that they themselves developed! In essence, they positioned themselves as a lame duck because they were afraid to encourage development of technology away from their bread and butter—photo film and print business.

Kodak highlights how imperative it is to your success to be willing to revise your corporate identity, harness the energy of disruption, not let fear paralyze your progress, and convert obstacles into opportunities.

The VICTORY Take-Away

There will forever be obstacles that line your path to success.

External obstacles cannot be controlled. However, through the continued use of the SWOT (strengths, weaknesses, opportunities and threats) analysis, you can prepare for potential threats and turn every obstacle into an opportunity.

Internal obstacles that threaten our inner thoughts and beliefs can be interrupted and changed through the tapping process. Our ability to overcome these obstacles is contingent upon maintaining a high level of motivation; by understanding our internal motivators, as opposed to external motivators, our stamina to work through our obstacles is increased.

It is important to remember that every successful person has experienced failure. How you choose to react to failure will dictate your success; be resilient, learn from your errors and move ahead!

Take Action

- Review your SWOT analysis, identifying any opportunities and threats that may create an obstacle. Create a plan to convert the obstacle into an opportunity.
- For every goal created to support your plan to drive your business to VICTORY, list any foreseeable obstacles, and then create a strategy to counteract the interference.
- Create a daily plan to boost your motivation to ensure that you are functioning at an optimal level.
- Identify your own personal internal obstacles that keep you from moving forward. Take action and combat your fears and challenges.

Post-Race: Cooling Down

SCAN TO VIEW POST-RACE VIDEO

chrisvanderzyden.com/cool-down

Chapter 6. Review, Revise, Re-Do

MISTAKES ARE INEVITABLE, and our errors are what push us to do better the next go-round. The bike portion of a tri is my favorite. As the longest leg of the race it allows me an opportunity to make up for lost time as I zigzag my way to the swim finish line.

It also happens to be my bliss. I love the hills, especially when I take out the men, mostly because they are heavier and not quite as compact as I am. However, I kid myself into thinking it is all a result of my superior technique!

The bike portion isn't always a smooth ride, though. One of my first lessons was to ensure that my bike is racked in the right gear—or actually in any gear at all.

In my very first triathlon I transitioned onto my bike to find that my chain had completely fallen off in transit. I had forgotten to check to be sure I was in the proper gear prior to the race. This is quite similar actually to launching your business without having done quite enough market research.

Another misfortune is to be flying down a hill nestled in your arrow bars, only to realize that on the other side you have an immediate steep incline, and you drop your chain as you madly downshift. Likewise, poor reaction to market changes can also hurt you in business.

Then there is drafting. Drafting is when a cyclist rides behind another cyclist and benefits from the lead cyclist's energy, creating an unfair advantage—definitely illegal. To avoid a drafting penalty, the cyclist merely needs to overtake the lead cyclist and swiftly pass them.

The same rule applies in business. If you want to win, you must distinguish yourself and take the lead.

Okay—you have officially launched your business. You have not only planned and created the strategy and supporting tactics to launch your business model, but you have actually executed.

All systems are in place. You are selling your product or service and making money. You have real customers and a marketing wheel in place that is sure to continue to drive customers. You have developed a motivated team that is engaged and committed to the business's success. You have made a few goals. Yes, now it is just one smooth race right?

Nope.

Business is done in a very dynamic environment, and unfortunately many companies have a powerful launch and then they ever so slowly slide into a chasm of complacency. They ignore the changes in their market and continue running things as usual, never taking a pulse on their progress.

By not taking a step back and reviewing how your business is performing, you will never be able to identify the gaps, the weaknesses, the lost revenue or the strengths that need to be leveraged.

So what happens when we stick our head in the sand? Things quickly become messy, margins slip, sales don't come in, employees become disenchanted and opportunities aren't capitalized upon.

To drive your business above and beyond your current production level, a reoccurring system of *reviewing* your analytics and progress, *revising* your strategy and *re-doing* will ensure your business continues to perform at the platinum level.

By reviewing the outcomes of each function, an assessment of strengths and weaknesses can be made in regards to the attainment of goals in each department.

In this chapter, we will discuss key performance indicators (KPIs) and review the tactics for each key segment of your business.

Review, Revise and Re-Do Your Marketing Metrics

I had a client once (or perhaps I had maybe hundreds of clients) who never looked at the analytics of an online marketing outreach program. They literally thought it was enough that they pushed send on their email marketing.

Your analytics are your gold! That is where the click-through rate is detailed, and the process of converting outreach into actual customers begins.

There are many tools to track your online results—and you don't have to hire a rocket scientist, be a statistician or pay a fortune.

A great website tool is Google Analytics. It is free and a must if you have a website. It allows you to view different metrics about your website traffic, such as how many people are visiting, how they are finding you, and what information is getting the most clicks and shares.

Another metric that needs to be tracked—and every business should be utilizing this channel to some degree—is social media. Google Analytics includes a social tab under "traffic sources." You want to track what social sites are driving traffic to your site: Facebook, Twitter, LinkedIn, Reddit, Google+, Hacker News, etc.

The point is to identify the sources your traffic is coming from and then revise your strategy to focus more of your marketing on the streams that produce the best results.

Another number to look at is click-through rates. Do the number of clicks correlate to conversion? I think so. Use bit.ly on social media and it will track your click-throughs. Want to keep track of your Twitter followers? Use TwitterCounter.

I have heard many clients question if social media is truly productive. It depends on your target audience and if they use social media. That being said, all business must have some presence on social media sites, if only for networking through LinkedIn. If you don't understand it, get your teenager—or someone's teenager—to help you.

If you are to be a successful entrepreneur you are going to have to engage in social media and watch the analytics. I have a company that watches over my social media for me—yes, it is one of the "delegates" for me, and it runs smoothly. I found that when I was trying to "do it all," social media was the one marketing tool that I left dragging, partly because I didn't fully understand it and also because I just didn't enjoy it. Some people love it, some don't—but either way, I can't think of any business that can get away with no social media presence at all.

If your marketing plan for your business incorporates a traditional marketing method, such as a direct-mailed promotional piece, track the results. How many did you send? How many recipients responded without a follow up? How many targets turned into real customers? How many outreaches post-campaign—and by what method (phone, email, physical meetings)—resulted in conversion?

Compute the return on investment of direct mail campaigns. How much did the promotional piece cost to produce? What was the response rate and sales produced?

Again, it is very simple. A business will become more profitable if results are consistently reviewed and strategies revised to incorporate more of what works and less of what doesn't.

Review, Revise and Re-Do Your Sales Data

Sales data analysis provides key performance indicators and will help you understand past results, revise sales strategies for the future, and provide guidance to forecast future expectations. An analysis contributes to understanding whether the sales goals and overall company growth goals are being met.

When my clients first start out, whether they are selling a product or service, I encourage them to review the sales numbers at the end of every business day. Review the sales by sales tapes, or if the business is a brick-and-mortar business, utilize your point-of-sale system, or simply keep a list in a desk drawer and write down the gross profit every time you sell.

When I started my first business, I did a hand-written list! This method gives a day-to-day outlook of how the business is performing. If the numbers are low, it will inspire you to take action to drive sales. If the daily number is high, it will encourage you to analyze why, so you can keep investing in what is producing the positive result.

Your sales analysis will guide you in recognizing what marketing channels and programs are producing the best results and which methods need to be revised to produce greater results.

Define what metrics of measure will provide the most valuable data, such as:

- Total sales in a given period of time. If sales have gone up, to what do you attribute the increase?
- How quickly do the targets entering the sales funnel move to customer status?
- What is driving the target to become a prospect and then a customer?

- Are your customers demographically stronger in one sector or another?
- Compute the average income of each order and the average income per unit. Is your sales volume up or did the average sale per unit increase?
- Identify trends in product categories. This will guide you to identify inventory slackers versus strong performing items.
- Assess cost of goods sold. If the cost is going up, is it in direct relation to sales volume, or does the number indicate that there would be a benefit from finding different resources that will provide quality material at a lower cost?

There are many tools to help you collect data. As I mentioned, one option is to manually track sales results, or access data through an accounting system, such as Quickbooks or a customer relationship management (CRM) system that will allow you to customize reports. A point-of-sale (POS) software system will provide data if the business is product-based.

It doesn't really matter what method is chosen, but it is important that the analysis is done on a consistent basis.

Review, Revise and Re-Do Your Customer Relations

Sales data also provides valuable insight to customer behavior and will give warning signs of impending trouble.

One of the top reasons for business failure is an inability to understand customers' needs. Understanding the needs and recognizing when customers' needs are changing is imperative to growing your customer base and profits.

A great method to identify changing customer needs is to simply send out a survey. It's not all about customer satisfaction (although this is an important measurement to gauge retention and referrals). A survey, whether informal or formal, can derive a temperature reading to discover new needs.

One of the benefits of a survey is that it allows your customers the freedom to express their thoughts and needs blindly, which tends to produce honest and useful information.

Step 1 – Choose a platform to conduct your survey.
There are many online programs. I have used SurveyMonkey.com and found their process to be affordable and easy.

Another option is SurveyGizmo.com, although they only offer a free trial. Otherwise, you need a paid account to use them.

Step 2 – Select the customers to be surveyed.
If the customer population is a small number, then survey the entire group. If, however, hundreds of customers are in the database, then choose a sample size across demographics to get a good read.

Step 3 – Create your survey.

Keep in mind that we do not want customers to feel burdened, so offer them something in return for participating, such as a discount code.

Before generating your questions, be clear on the purpose of your survey. What type of information do you want to gain? Quality of service, speed of service, type of service or product, pricing or general problems are a few options to focus upon. And remember, the fewer the questions the better.

AT&T recently surveyed me via text. I thought that was terrific as it was quick and easy. They asked five questions, all yes/no answers or on a scale of 1-10.

Mobile surveying is immediately engaging, so the response rate will be high in comparison to a written survey. Just be sure to ask the right type of questions.

If it is possible, get out there and go see your customers, as there is no better feedback than a face-to-face review. By being very personalized you will derive more detailed information about the concerns of your customers and what they like best about your product or service.

I have found that in a face-to-face conversation most customers are more than willing to explain what is working and what is not, and it is an opportunity to really drill down and assess the needs of your customer.

Don't use this precious time as a sales call, but be aware that it is an opportunity to further promote how you can be of support in the future.

Measuring your customer's satisfaction level with your product and service is crucial—and you don't want to hear that they are just satisfied. You need them to be, in Ken Blanchard and Sheldon Bowles' words, "raving fans." (If you haven't read their book, the title is *Raving Fans: A Revolutionary Approach to Customer Service.* You can find it online at chrisvanderzyden.com/RavingFans.) Discern the level of praise—it is really important!

The bottom line is your customers are the driving force to your sales and profitability. And selling to an existing customer is five times more profitable. Finding a new customer is expensive and time-consuming, so be sure your existing customers are raving!

Review, Revise and Re-Do Your Financial Statements

The financial statements are one of the greatest tools to identify weaknesses in a business. The numbers never lie and will alert when trouble is brewing, giving time to be proactive in resolving issues. Is there a problem in your inventory control? Do cash management procedures need to be tightened? Is pricing out of whack? Are operating expenses skewed?

Carefully and consistently analyze the financial statements, watch the trends and compare period-to-period. This effort will guide to better management decisions that will positively impact the bottom line. Trust me—it pays to fall in love with the numbers, and you don't have to be a CPA to understand them and utilize them to your advantage.

The fact of the matter is that most people are scared of numbers. I have watched very brilliant small business owners go down in flames because, other than signing their tax return at the end of the year, they never looked at their financials. Or they trusted another to oversee their financial statements only to be embezzled from.

According to the Small Business Administration, one-third of new businesses fail within two years, and 56% within the first four years.

I actually thought these stats were pretty good—two-thirds stay in business for two years—not bad at all! But, how many are profitable? Only about 40%.

Why the lack of profits and thus the high failure rate? The primary inadequacies cited are 1) incompetence and 2) lack of financial knowledge.

I get it. The finance side of business is just not as sexy as the product development, marketing and sales, or whatever is your sweet spot in your business. However, it is critical to success that the financial information is not only understood but also utilized to make sound management decisions.

Hire a CPA and a bookkeeper to do the dirty work, but do not hide your head in the sand in regards to what your financial picture looks like.

In chapter three under the finance pillar, detailed information was presented as to how to understand your financial statements. To recap, here are a few key indicators to continuously review when revising your business plan:

Current Ratio – the ratio of current assets to current liabilities. *Current assets* are those assets that can be converted to cash within the current period, such as accounts receivable. *Current liabilities* are those liabilities that are expected to be paid off within a current year, such as accounts payable.

Computed: Current Assets / Current Liabilities

A 2:1 ratio (twice the assets as liabilities) is a good marker of a healthy small business.

Inventory turnover – the number of times that inventory is replaced in a period. This provides an indicator of how well the inventory levels are being managed.

Computed: Cost of Goods Sold (CGS found on the income statement) / Average Inventory in a Given Period

Analyze if your rate is good. How is it trending compared to previous periods? Compare your turnover rate to your successful competitors.

Receivables turnover – the measurement of how many times a business collects its receivables in a period, or how efficient their collection process is. The goal is to collect receivables as quickly as possible, so the higher the ratio the better.

Computed: Credit Sales / Average Accounts Receivable

Gross Profit Margin = (Sales – CGS) / Revenue

Analyze and assess if you are making a profit on the products you are selling.

Operating Profit Margin = (Revenue – Operating Expenses) / Revenue

This will indicate how efficiently your company is operating.

Net Profit Margin = Net Income/Revenue

This is the income derived from every dollar of revenue.

And don't forget to review your budget. Investigate the variances in your projections and revise as necessary.

Review, Revise and Re-Do Your Team

Ever have the experience of losing a key employee or team member? There is nothing like that sinking feeling of "Oh s**t! How am I ever going to find that kind of talent again?"

The fact of the matter is that attrition hurts a company. The expense of attracting new team members and the time investment required to nurture them into engaging and highly productive employees is immense.

The big question is: Does your corporate culture make for a happy environment?

I had a five-million dollar a year client who had created a new product line in response to an unfilled need in the market that came about as a result of a new regulation.

As often is the case, this new product line required new employees and team leaders. As they assimilated the new talent into the existing the organization, the culture shifted and a large part of the team became dissatisfied because of the changing compensation plan.

The leaders of the company were unaware of the shift until they lost several key employees. That is actually the point at which they reached out to me. They were caught by surprise to learn of the dissatisfaction and unsure how to correct the downhill slide of employee distrust that was threatening the success of their new product.

Again, your employees are your greatest assets. Just like your products you need to pay attention to what is working and what is not.

If you are unsure and have more than a handful of team members, utilize an employee satisfaction survey. Gallup is one of the leading developers of employee surveys. This will provide you with invaluable feedback and ensure that your key assets are happy and performing at their highest level.

In addition, invest in each employee by performing employee reviews at specified periods. Don't make this an annual program—stay in touch with your employees more frequently and you will stay ahead of concerns that can contribute to a high attrition rate.

A review is not about giving an employee a pass or fail grade. Yes, more formal reviews are about documenting successes and deficiencies, addressing compensation and promotion. But, it is also an opportunity to give quality feedback and mentoring that can inspire achievement.

The employee-employer relationship has changed to one of true mutual benefit. In order to retain employees an employer must be actively engaged in developing the employee.

Reviews provide a specified time to focus on each employee and give guidance in setting and reviewing goals, establishing a plan to achieve the goals, and identifying criteria to define their success. Reviews are just a conversation and, if performed well, will give valuable information about strengths and weaknesses in the organization and will go a long way towards developing employees to achieve at their highest level.

Again, if the focus is on supporting and developing team members, listening to their concerns and comments, and making changes as necessary, a loyal and high-achieving community can be developed.

Another relationship aspect to review, beyond your internal organization, is a review of strategic partners who are external to your business. Strategic partnerships are companies or people who drive business—referral partners. They are associates who perhaps have complementary businesses that share a common target audience. For example, a CPA's possible strategic partners are attorneys, insurance agents, financial planners, investment advisors, etc.

Referral partners are avenues that are utilized to cross-promote each other. Strategic partnerships should be reviewed to determine which associations are most successful in referring business.

By identifying what channels are most productive, a review can then be performed to narrow specific actions that were undertaken to drive referrals. Then you can further collaborate and create a marketing plan for the future.

Cross-marketing through specific referral partners is a great strategy, and it doesn't have to be another business—it can be an association or anyone who has a list of people who match your target list. For example, I had a client who was writing a book that would benefit the medical field. We researched specific medical associations with members who would benefit from the information within the book. We then offered to give members of the association a free chapter, and this strategy drove book sales.

The association benefited by having great information to pass onto their members, and my client benefitted by creating awareness of her book.

Strategic partnerships are win-win scenarios for both sides of the equation, so it is a mutually beneficial strategy that is really powerful.

Review, Revise and Re-Do Your Operations

Assess how efficiently the business is operating. How well the objectives of the business are being met will give insight as to the organization's efficacy and will identify holes that are potentially leaking profits.

Review the facility the business is operating in to determine if it meets the needs of the business. Is the rent and location appropriate? Does the space provide efficiency in production of goods?

Are your hours of operation working? I once had a dentist who discovered he needed to have a late night to accommodate his patients who couldn't schedule appointments during the day. A simple shift to offering late night Wednesdays increased his production.

Does equipment need to be upgraded, or do suppliers need to be expanded?

Is the production lead-time meeting your customers' expectations?

All of these questions will provide direction to uncover any inefficiencies that need to be corrected.

Review, Revise and Re-Do Your Personal Goals

Be steadfast in reviewing your progress towards achieving your goals on a daily basis, and don't confuse activity for achievement. Your personal and business success depends upon your commitment to take meaningful action on a daily basis that produces results.

The only way to assess the progress being made is to review the action plan you have created daily and honestly assess if the business is progressing at the desired rate.

It is important to monitor your progress, but also to assess your enjoyment of the process. Attaining the goals is important, but it is just as important to enjoy the process. If you are not fulfilled in the action of moving toward your goals, your motivation will slip.

The VICTORY Take-Away

Continuously *reviewing* the processes, strategies and tactics that support the goals of a business will provide guidance to the necessary *revisions* required to ensure the business functions at an optimal level. Persistence in *re-doing* will drive growth and profits, and create sustained success. Review, revise, re-do.

Take Action

- Create a review system and define key indicators and metrics of success for all operations within the business at specific intervals.
- Revise the action plan of strategies and tactics for each pillar as necessary.
- Re-do and execute your revised plan, and then…review, revise and re-do again.

Chapter 7. Hanging with the Yeasayers

WHAT IS THE ULTIMATE KEY to success? The answer lies in your ability to master your thoughts.

The last leg of a triathlon is always the run. At this point, the competitors have exhausted their upper body with the swim and their lower body with the cycling. The race culminates with merging their upper and lower body with a nice long run. Long, but hopefully not too slow.

This is the opportunity in the race when an athlete has a chance to assess what they are truly made of. Most often the race is held during a beautiful time of year, which makes for a lovely swim and hopefully a dry, warm cycle.

However, by the time you get to the run portion, typically it is mid-day with the sun blazing. Grueling is the word that comes to my mind as the battle rages with a hill in ninety-degree weather and 90% humidity. This is the moment when an athlete leans in and utilizes not their muscles, but their mind.

Great athletes understand that their mindset will determine their success just as much if not more than their physical performance. This applies to our businesses as well. Whether you choose to exercise a positive or negative mindset impacts the success of your business and your bottom line.

I learned very early in life that my mind was a powerful instrument. When I was younger, I was a ten-meter springboard diver with a professional team, performing exhibitions in Europe and, quite frankly, I was lacking in ability in comparison to my teammates. My coach would teach me a new dive first on the trampoline, and then I would move it to the board. Of course, this was done for safety so I would remain in one piece and not kill myself trying everything new from the board first time out.

I, however, understood the power of the mind and knew that my greatest practice would occur while I was sitting in the bleachers with a towel over my head practicing the new dive over and over in my mind.

Although my teammates would tease me for my inactive practice style, it worked! I could learn a new dive in my mind by my memorizing how the dive looked, how I felt with every position in the air, how the air felt around me as I launched from the board.

I would visually practice where the sky would be in every turn, what the timing was as I came out of the dive, what the water felt like as my hands cut the water, and how I would tuck and roll the dive as soon as I entered the water.

Mindset of Success

This is the power of the mind. Use your mind to practice logistics, but more importantly, practice how your success *feels* in your mind.

Exercising a positive or negative mindset impacts the success of whatever sport you enjoy, and will also impact your business and bottom line.

Utilizing your mind to create the success you desire is just as important as the other factors of your business. Ultimately, the best sales and marketing strategy will not make up for a lack of having developed a mindset of success.

In this final chapter, you will learn how to master a mindset of success and develop your own tribe of yeasayers. We'll talk about networking, the power of a mastermind group, and the benefits of being a mentor and a mentee.

I feel the "Y" in VICTORY is the most important in your blueprint to operating your business at the platinum level. Enjoy.

You Are Your Biggest, Most Important Yeasayer

How do we cultivate a mindset of success? The first step is to be aware of your thought processes. Remember, you and only you can control your thoughts. Thus your level of success is 100% within your power.

This is great news. You own your success or failure. It is all up to you—and choosing to develop a positive mindset is as easy as strengthening a muscle.

Most people move through life with absolutely no awareness of their thoughts and spend precious little time indulging in self-introspection. But, the reality is there will be little improvement in our businesses and lives if we don't take the time to evaluate our weaknesses and strengths. The first step toward elevating our mindset is to understand the quality of our thoughts. Are we powerful in attracting greatness into our life, or are we repelling the positive with our negative thought process?

Some have said that our disposition is engrained into us like our DNA and we are positive or negative depending on our genetics. I don't buy into this fatalistic belief system.

We all control our thoughts and have the ability to train ourselves to shift our mindset to positive, and we can do it on a dime!

"The mind is a terrible thing to waste." ~ **Forest Long**

Three Steps to Mastering a Mindset of Success

How powerful is our mind? Well, our mind cannot envision a negative command. True.

Have you ever had the experience of yelling to a child, "Don't slam the door!" and inevitably the door is slammed? Now think about it—what do you envision in your head when you hear, "Don't slam the door!"? You picture a door slamming. That is why it never works to give negative direction hoping for a positive outcome.

Now try, "Please, gently close the door." Can you envision a door closing quietly? Bingo. Thus, the power of the mind.

Or, how about this one—you are waiting for a project or signed contract to come in or an email from a special friend. While waiting you are thinking you will be rejected, the project will sour, they gave the contract to someone else. You allow yourself to experience all of these negative scenarios in your mind. But then, the much-anticipated email drops into your inbox and you immediately perk up. You haven't even read the email, and for all you know the worst-case scenarios that you have conjured up in your mind while waiting for a response may in fact be the reality, yet you are lifted just by the very sight of a response appearing in your inbox.

We are naturally hopeful and lean towards the positive. This is an example of how quickly our mind can shift our thoughts.

Success begins with our thoughts, and a mindset of success is a choice.

Our thoughts feed our mind, and our mind projects our reality. In short, we create our own success or failures. How is that for self-responsibility?

If you are not happy with your level of success in your business and your life, it is time to assess the quality of your thoughts and begin to cultivate a positive mindset. And yes, as an added bonus, a positive mindset will translate into a positive bottom line in your business.

A positive mindset creates motivation, increases productivity and creativity, and unlocks the presentation of opportunity. The return on investment of a positive mindset, while I recognize cannot be computed, is exponential.

Your success as an entrepreneur hinges on your ability to master a positive mindset and also instill in your team a positive mindset.

The three steps that will guide you to develop and nurture a positive mindset include:

1. **Identify your personal weakness for destructive thinking.** What is the dominant force that is holding you back from succeeding? Our thought process is developed through our experiences within our families, schools, communities and society in general.

    We develop our mindset from our negative or positive experiences, and as a result we may create obstacles in our thought process. We can, however, retrain the way we process this information into a positive position.

    For example, an individual has an experience of giving a presentation in school that was not well received by their classmates and that pain of rejection created in their mind the thought that they are not able to effectively present. A negative thought process and judgment about their ability to give a presentation has been created. That negative mindset prohibits them from believing in their ability to sell, and now they have an obstacle that keeps them from developing the business they deserve.

    Or, perhaps a child with a learning difficulty in a particular area experiences an interaction with an unenlightened teacher that defines the child as being dumb. That child then gives power to that message, and it fuels a negative self-perception that, if unattended, forever hinders his ability to succeed.

Our cultures and families contribute to our positive or negative mindset with their messages. Think about some of the common messages we receive as children: money doesn't grow on trees, life is hard, etc. These messages become engrained in our minds and translated as limiting beliefs, such as there is not abundance, life is supposed to be difficult, and so on. But in reality there is enough abundance for everyone to be successful, and life does not have to be hard. Life is as abundant and as easy as we make it.

A few common mindset obstacles are:

A. Restricted thinking – all the beliefs that prevent us from achieving our true desires. Common themes are: "I'm not smart, I don't know what I'm doing, I don't have enough money to do what I want to do, I don't know what to do or what order to do it in." This is the little voice in our head that tells us we "can't." Restricted thinking is unfortunately planted in our heads from a very young age when our parents begin to tell us "no" during our formative years. Of course these admonishments are done in an effort to keep us safe as we reach for hot stoves, etc., but unfortunately the negative becomes engrained in our minds and creates restricted thinking that keeps us from attaining the level of success that we are capable of achieving.

B. Results attachment – our thoughts are attached to a particular result, as opposed to the process of achievement. When we are overly attached to the result, we are more likely to give up when we don't attain our goals at the level or within the time frame desired. Keep shifting the action, attaching the action to the process, not to the end result—this allows for adjustments in strategies and the continuation to progress forward. Remember, it is all a journey to be enjoyed, and as I mentioned before in the previous discussion about failures, Henry Ford persisted because he was devoted to the process of inventing the car, not to the result of achieving. That is how he reached his success.

C. Victim mindset – not taking self-responsibility—blaming others for preventing you from getting what you want. "Nobody in my family is ever successful, that is just the way it is." Concluding that the lack of success is a result of circumstances that are beyond our control, or the result of some other exterior force, is a demonstration of shifting responsibility away from where it belongs—with oneself. Taking responsibility for your own thoughts is equivalent to owning your success and failures. The victim mindset is most common and will forever hinder the ability to achieve success in business. Choose to change it!

D. Problem-focus thinking – focusing on the problem and not on a solution. Engaging in tunnel vision that is problem-focused prohibits the recognition that creative solutions exist. Keeping the focus fixated on the future and solutions, not on the problems in the past, will move your mindset to the positive.

E. Dwelling on negative feelings – negative feelings create walls to achieve. Negative feelings attract negativity. It is as simple as that.

2. **Create a shift in your mindset from negative to positive.**

   A. Create a new belief – Identify your personal negative self-talk and create a new belief to counteract the negative. Forget negative past experiences and program yourself to believe a new story. "I am smart," "I am talented," and "I am successful."

   There are two types of beliefs:

   1. **Untrue beliefs** – These are beliefs that are *mis*interpretations of past events and not reality.
   2. **Replacement beliefs** – These are *re*interpretations of old events and associated beliefs. This is the process of reevaluating past experiences at a deeper level and, as an adult, consciously deciding to understand the negative and uncover the positive in the event in order to reframe your belief.

B. Abandon and release – Reinterpret the old event in a new way. For example, the school told you that you were stupid and you actually had dyslexia. Many people today have experienced "labeling," in which a child has been deemed challenged or stupid only to become amazingly successful. Successful people are able to understand the labeling in a new way. For example, they create a new understanding that the school didn't have the knowledge to understand those educational challenges at that time, and they abandon the "story," release the label and replace the thought with "I am smart. I just learn in a different way." Getting a wider view of past events and reinterpreting the event to create a new belief is a powerful antidote in shifting a negative mindset to a positive one.

3. **Reinforce your new belief system.**

    A. Acknowledge and release the fear – Visualize powerful, successful thoughts. Athletes utilize this technique often. Visualization is mental practice prior to execution.

    B. Be mindful of your tribe or circle of influencers – Limit, as best you can, negative naysayers, or as I like to refer to them—the dream stealers.

    C. Affirmations – Create and utilize powerful statements written in the now.

    D. Draw on past successes – As mentioned earlier, make a list of all of the great things you have accomplished. When you become doubtful as to your abilities, pull out that list and review.

Nurture a mindset of success and it will pay dividends in the success of your business.

Remember the actor Michael J. Fox in the sitcom *Family Ties* wearing a suit and carrying a briefcase as a kid? The character in that show was a great example of nurturing a mindset of success. Think it, act it, be it, expect it. "It" is success.

Develop a Tribe of Yeasayers

Your tribes are your "people." Your people will drive you to a higher level or they can take you down. They are the people with whom you communicate, whom you depend on for advice and offer you feedback on your progress or lack of progress. These are the people you trust.

Successful people hang out with successful people. That is because they share a common belief system. Successful people like to share ideas, are focused on their goals, and therefore have conversations that are geared towards the positive end of the spectrum.

Conversely, people who feel challenged and hopeless to achieve a higher level of success tend to surround themselves with like-minded people. Misery loves company, right? They can share their complaints about the world and how they are mistreated, and nobody in the group is going to talk about self-responsibility. The negative talk is secure, and a never-ending, self-fulfilling swirl of failure.

Your circle of friends dictate your level of exposure to positive or negative conversations and ideas, and can ultimately drive your level of income and how happy you are. Many financial advisors have made the observation that your income level, in most cases, is the average of your five closest friends. Of course, you will always have friends that are your "true" friends regardless of income level. However, the financial success of your circle of influence can have a powerful impact on your level of success.

Migrate to a positive, higher level and you will recognize that the conversations are different—and you may find that it is easier to attain the level of success you desire.

But, how do we create a tribe? Be choosy and conscious about the people with whom you associate. We have only so much time, so spend it wisely with people who have the same level of interest in success as you.

I know that you are interested in success or you wouldn't have hung in there and gotten to chapter seven of this VICTORY book!

If you are not at the level of achievement that you expect and you realize that your associations are lacking, change them. Edit the people in your life and trade up to be with people you want to be more like.

Networking

Networking is a great avenue to identify people with whom you have a common interest. Successful people understand the benefits of networking in guiding them to achieve what they want in their business. Developing a network can be done in person by joining associations in your industry, chamber meetings, alumni associations or charity foundations.

Your network doesn't have to be directly tied to your business—you may be a foodie and decide to join a culinary network. Diversity of networks will ensure that you meet different people in different industries, which will provide more exposure.

Virtual networking is also a great channel for networking. LinkedIn offers terrific online networking groups that are easy to find and engage with.

A few guidelines regarding networking and building a tribe:

1. **Be generous** – Networking is about having a forum in which to give and nurture relationships. If you approach networking as an opportunity to help other people, you will naturally attract people who want to give to you. It is a mutually beneficial relationship. With the right attitude, your network will naturally expand and be productive.

2. **Be trustworthy** – Always network with the highest integrity. Networking is not a place to "sell" your product or service. Networking is about engaging on a productive level and being genuine.

3. **Always deliver** – This is about being authentic and true to your word. Without fail, always deliver on your promises. Even if it is as simple as an offer of introduction to a colleague, be sure to execute upon any offers.

4. **Follow up** – This goes hand-in-hand with delivering. After a networking opportunity, be sure to follow up with those people with whom you have identified a similarity. Stay connected by sending a personal note or email and by inviting them to link with you on LinkedIn. A strong follow-up will ensure that your relationships continue to grow, and from that referrals may blossom.

The tribe you develop will help you troubleshoot your challenges. They will celebrate your successes, they will motivate you, and they will inspire you.

Your tribe will influence how enjoyable and successful your journey is. So be sure you have exactly who you want to become in your tribe!

Masterminds

"Whatever the mind can conceive and believe, the mind can achieve."

~ Napoleon Hill

The definition of a *mastermind,* per Napoleon Hill:

Two or more people who work in perfect harmony for the attainment of a definite purpose.

Napoleon Hill was a great American author and esteemed thought leader in the personal development arena. His work in examining and evangelizing the power of our personal beliefs upon our level of success is widely acclaimed. His most successful book, *Think and Grow Rich*, is one of the best-selling personal development books of all time. He was a strong advocate of the benefits of a mastermind group. (Find it online at chrisvanderzyden.com/ThinkAndGrowRich.)

The benefit of a mastermind group is that it provides an association of members that are focused on helping each other achieve whatever it is they desire. It provides a venue of safety to freely express challenges and seek assistance from others who possibly have more experience and can offer insight as to possible solutions that you have not been able to identify.

By forming an alliance with a mastermind group, you have the ability to leverage each other's experiences, influence, and insight, which will guide you to achieve your goals quicker, and most likely with less pain than if you were doing it on your own.

I have been a member of a formal mastermind group in which we paid dues and met in different cities throughout the United States. The members of this group were all high-level business professionals. We would meet for several days in a conference room at a hotel and brainstorm various ways to elevate each of our businesses.

It was challenging to develop solutions for other businesses, but at the same time the process guides the participants to see their own businesses in a different light.

Within the confines of a mastermind group you are stretched beyond your comfort zone and are driven to release your own creative thoughts.

It was brilliant, and I will say that I learned more from that group than any other professional experience I have had in my life.

In one year, my business catapulted to a height that I am sure I would not have been quite as successful achieving on my own. I have worked with people like Jack Canfield that I would have never worked with before if not for my mastermind group.

I would not have created the strategies to create the business I wanted without my group. I would not have been so brave in my pursuit of success. I would not have been as creative in my solutions.

Thanks to Jeff Hayzlett, I am now more comfortable with the tension of being uncomfortable than ever before. My group taught me that tension is the precursor to launch, and I understand that now.

I can personally attest to the fact that the benefits of a mastermind group are tremendous.

I have also been a participant in an informal mastermind group. Informal groups can be comprised of local people that you meet with in person, or they can be done virtually.

I lead a mastermind group that spans three continents and, truly, the only challenge in scheduling the meetings is the myriad of time zones.

I am a real proponent of crowd-sourcing solutions to challenges in the pursuit of fulfilling our dreams and, to that end, I encourage participating in or creating a mastermind group.

And like the four Ps of marketing, here are my four Ps to developing a powerful and productive mastermind tribe:

1. **Purpose** – Be crystal clear as to the vision of the group. Define the common denominator and purpose of the group as a whole, and the intended outcome for the participants. Is the purpose for business development? Is it to raise awareness of a global issue? Is it to lose weight? The focus can be for any purpose—it is most important that the members be in alignment with the intent of the group.

2. **People** – Be strategic in selecting people for participation. The best mastermind groups have people who have a variety of expertise so that each person is a resource for different information. Look for people who are committed, determined to succeed, thoughtful, and of the highest integrity.

   This group will bond in a big way and will form a safe place to share weaknesses, along with strengths, so you want to be sure the members will be sensitive, insightful and hold the information in confidence. You can identify potential members in your associations or within your online community.

3. **Place** – Your meetings can be hosted online through Skype, freeconferencecall.com or, if you want to share information on a screen, I use GoToMeeting.com. If possible, meetings in person allow for the development of great synergy within the group. Depending on the nature and format of the group, meetings are typically held weekly, monthly or quarterly. The key to

establishing a successful group is to develop consistency in the meetings and to be sure that each member understands the importance of committing to the group.

4. **Protocol** – One person will typically lead the group, and the leader can change from meeting-to-meeting if this works for the group. It is beneficial to have a person who has facilitator experience so that time is well spent. The basic format is to give each member a period of time to express their successes during the week, and acknowledge the challenges that they are seeking help in overcoming. The members of the group can then offer assistance or advice.

At the conclusion of the meeting each member will commit to achieving certain goals prior to the next meeting. This ensures that there is momentum going forward and creates a system of accountability to themselves and members of the group.

Preparation of notes during the meeting is essential to memorialize challenges, commitments and contributions. Post-meeting, the notes should be sent to remind all members of the challenges that members are working toward overcoming, and to establish a system of accountability for the members.

Finding a Lead Yeasayer – A Mentor

Mentor relationships come in many different forms. Most of us have experienced a mentor relationship. Some are through a formal agreement and some we are just lucky to stumble upon.

I have had many mentors who have guided me, and for many different reasons. I attribute my success to having had the benefit of many mentors who so generously passed their experiences down to me.

When I was a CPA with PriceWaterhouseCoopers, I formed a professional mentorship with a partner in the firm. He was in his eighties at the time and had a wealth of information to share. I've had mentors for running, triathlons and parenting too. A mentor is merely a person who shares their wisdom and helps pave the path to success for their mentee.

The most significant benefit of having a mentor is the time saved by being able to draw on the experience of a mentor.

Time is our most valuable asset. Why waste time fumbling for answers when someone with more experience and wisdom can shorten our path to success?

The guidance a mentor provides is invaluable. The benefit of this relationship is not one-sided, however, but in fact is mutually beneficial. A mentor is afforded the opportunity to improve leadership skills and is provided the satisfaction of helping someone move closer to their success.

Many times, an entrepreneur will be inspired by watching another business or colleague's success and wonder: How did they do it?

Ask them. More often than not, successful people are more than happy to help someone who is starting out. Successful people are inclined to bring other people forward, so just ask. Invite them for coffee and ask great questions and explore the potential for a mentor-mentee relationship.

Here are a few ground rules to ensure the development of an effective and mutually beneficial mentorship:

1. Identify an individual in your industry who has excelled, exhibits a similar value system, and is trustworthy and willing to share his/her knowledge. This person should inspire you towards achievement. Great mentors are skilled listeners, offer direction, and are particularly astute in interpreting your particular challenges and deficits. Approach the individual with clarity as to what you are expecting from the relationship (the information or specific skills you would like assistance in developing). I have mentioned this in previous sections and this applies once again. Surround yourself with positive people whom you admire.

2. Be cognizant that this relationship, although mutually beneficial, is most likely more to your favor, so in light of that fact be exceedingly clear with expectations and extremely respectful of your mentor's time. Formulate what will work for both of you. I have actually asked someone to speak to me every Friday for just 10 minutes in order to get a response on two questions. This individual was in high demand and I wanted to be enormously respectful of his time. My efficiency ultimately paid off for me, and I'm sure benefited him, if only in that it made him feel good to know he was helpful in guiding me to the next level.

3. As a mentee, it is up to you to get the most out of the relationship. Be clear in your questions, be gracious in receiving criticism, do the work as best you can, and learn from your mistakes. A successful mentorship requires a desire to succeed, and a bit of courage to be honest with yourself and your mentor about your shortcomings.

The VICTORY Take-Away

Avoiding the obstructionists who threaten to derail your success and choosing to hang out with the yeasayers will have a powerful impact on your ability to reach VICTORY in your business.

Master a positive mindset and you will inspire your team to do the same. Positive attracts positive, and once you embrace the natural trajectory of a positive mindset, success will be yours. I know that is a big statement, but if you take that one thought away from this book and take action on that sentiment, you will succeed.

Take Action

- Identify the obstacles in your thought process and create a strategy to shift any negative thoughts that are hindering your progress.
- Review your tribe and edit negative influencers out of your circle. Identify three avenues to expand your circle of influence to a higher level through networking.
- Join or create a mastermind group.

- Find a mentor to help pave your way to success—and likewise, be a mentor.

The Finish Line

YOU HAVE REACHED THE FINISH LINE and what is sure to be VICTORY for your business!

Entrepreneurship is a road to greater fulfillment, ease and wealth creation. There has never been in our history such a plethora of resources available to make owning your own business a possibility. If, from reading this book, you have established that entrepreneurship is a fit for you and your core values, then go for it.

Realize that the journey to entrepreneurial success is a marathon. It is not a sprint, and there truly are no shortcuts. Entrepreneurship is not a road to instant wealth but a path toward realizing new heights of success, both professionally and personally.

By utilizing the information in this book and creating your own personal roadmap, you will create the business that you deserve and desire.

The over-arching message of The VICTORY Code is to consistently take action in every stage of the race. Be sure that in your pre-race you have a clear vision and understand the gap that you will fill in the market. Test your business model and create a solid, actionable business plan. Remember, your business plan is a living document, meaning it is meant to be continuously reviewed and updated to ensure your business thrives.

On race day, launch every pillar of your business with strategies and tactics that will ensure you win. Ensure your business is operating efficiently. Market your value proposition in a way that speaks your brand. Differentiate your product or service in a way that will make you stand out from the competition. Be sure your sales funnel is continuously flowing and creating raving customers. Utilize your financial information to make sound business decisions as you grow. Develop a team that is a solid and cohesive group. Employ technology in your organization to increase efficiency as well as to expand your business beyond your physical boundaries.

Be the leader of your organization, and set goals. Be aware of the internal and external obstacles that threaten the achievement of your goals, and engage the tools provided to overcome any challenges.

Post-race, clinch your VICTORY and protect your success by continuously reviewing, revising and re-doing—this will guard against bonking in the marathon and will make certain that your business continues to win.

And chapter seven—the gold in this book. Continuously practice a mindset of success. Develop a tribe of yeasayers who will support you through thick and thin. Network to find your tribe. Join a mastermind group, or create one. Be a mentor and a mentee.

You are strong enough to succeed. Activate the knowledge in this book and enjoy your VICTORY!

For the companion self-study action plan to develop your personal entrepreneurial VICTORY Code, please visit: www.chrisvanderzyden.com.

I want to know about your progress. Connect with me.

Twitter: https://twitter.com/chrisVNDRZYDN

Facebook: http://www.facebook.com/chrisVANDERZYDEN.com

LinkedIn: www.linkedin.com/in/chrisvanderzyden

Appendix A. Core Value Exercise

THE FIRST STEP TOWARDS creating your vision is to identify your personal four core values.

Below are five questions and a list of words that will guide you in identifying what values are most important to you. Answer the questions and digest the information thoroughly. You may want to work with a trusted friend to help you.

After you have answered the questions take your time as you read through the words and circle those words that resonate with who you are.

Refrain from circling words that you feel compelled to choose based on what you think other people expect of you. This exercise is intended to guide you to identify the core values that drive your decisions.

1. What are the top three successes in my life?

2. What three experiences have proven to be the most difficult for me?

3. What traits do I value in my closest friends?

4. What traits do I despise in others?

5. What positive qualities do people recognize in me the most?

Accountable	Capacity	Coordinate
Acknowledgment	Captivate	Counsel
Abundance	Caring	Creativity
Active	Caretaker	Credible
Adapt	Challenge	Crusade
Affinity	Champion	Cultivate
Affluence	Charisma	Curious
Agitate	Charm	Daring
Allegiance	Chance	Data
Amusement	Clarify	Develop
Animate	Class	Devise
Appease	Collect	Devotion
Arouse	Collaborate	Devout
Assert	Combine	Dexterity
Assist	Command	Diligence
Association	Communication	Dictate
Attachment	Competent	Discover
Attempt	Composed	Discretion
Authentic	Comprehend	Discriminate
Authority	Consciousness	Disturbance
Aware	Consistency	Dominate
Backbone	Consolidate	Drive
Blend	Conspire	Earn
Boost	Contribute	Ecstasy
Brilliance	Converge	Elation
Brainstorm	Convince	Embrace

Empower	Goodness	Metaphysical
Enchant	Gratification	Mindful
Enhance	Harmonious	Motivate
Enjoyment	Happiness	Natural
Enterprise	Hazard	Network
Entertainment	Humanity	Observant
Enthusiasm	Impact	Opportunity
Envision	Impartial	Peril
Ethical	Implication	Persist
Exceed	Impulsive	Pioneer
Exclusive	Incite	Pious
Expedite	Individuality	Pivot
Explore	Influence	Prestige
Expressive	Innovation	Process
Extreme	Insight	Procedure
Fantasy	Intention	Produce
Fearless	Intrigue	Professional
Finesse	Join	Progressive
Flash	Jubilation	Promote
Flexibility	Kindle	Propel
Flux	Knowing	Prosperity
Forceful	Laughter	Quality
Fulfill	Leader	Reciprocate
Fuse	Lenient	Refine
Galvanize	Light-hearted	Regulate
Generate	Love	Reinforce
Gentleness	Loyalty	Relate
Giggle	Lucid	Representative
Give	Manipulate	Respectful
Genuine	Mentor	Requirements

Revolutionize	Speculate	Thin-skinned
Result	Splendor	Thorough
Reveal	Stamina	Tranquility
Reverence	Start	Train
Reward	Stimulating	Truth
Riches	Study	Trustworthy
Sacred	Sustenance	Vigilant
Safety	Symmetry	Vision
Savor	Sympathetic	Wit
Sensitive	Territory	

Acknowledgements

FIRST AND FOREMOST, I thank every client that I have had the great pleasure of working with, as you were the true inspiration for this book.

And I thank you, the reader, for taking action and buying this book as a guide to bring your business to a higher level. It is a very noisy world, and discerning what information will produce a positive impact on our business is challenging. My hope is that you will utilize this book and implement the information provided to drive your business to new heights. As I said in the beginning, success is yours if you choose it— and take action!

I also want to acknowledge the members of my amazing mastermind groups: The Ritz Group, The Muses and my Bali Group. I am grateful and will be forever inspired by each very talented member. Each of you have motivated me, challenged me and provoked me to achieve. We have learned, laughed and loved together. I love all my tribes! Thank you all - XO.

Then there is the team who drove this book right into production: Eric Seplowitz, my amazingly patient sounding board and project manager; Betsy Phelps Seplowitz, my proofreader and grammar queen; Kelly Fermoyle, my content and line editor; Brenda Shih, my graphic designer and creative force; and Chris Westfall with Marie Street Press, my wonderful publishing house. I'd also like to thank the folks at

The Canfield Training Group—specifically John Beaman. Literally, it could not have been done without all of you.

Then there is my dream team…my daughters Carling and Lillie who put up with my travel schedule and the rock I hide under in my office as I work away doing what I love.

I thank my very large and supportive family and my friends who have so tirelessly listened to the development of The VICTORY Code—Lisa, Liz, Andrea, Karin, Mike, Betsy, Thea, Alex, Tara, Laura and many others.

About the Author

CHRIS VANDERZYDEN is a small business advocate, CPA, sales trainer, keynote speaker and creator of the 7 Step VICTORY Programs™ Her career began as a certified public accountant with Coopers & Lybrand, now PricewaterhouseCoopers. She then became a corporate defector and recreated her life as an entrepreneur and developed a nationwide advertising specialty and marketing company into a million dollar venture.

As a speaker, Chris delivers energetic, action-packed presentations filled with fresh concepts and essential strategies that inspire her audience to take action and achieve new levels of success. She is a recognized leader and is in demand to provide presentations to audiences ranging from 50 to 2,000 to many groups and audiences worldwide.

She is a highly sought-after broadcast commentator who has appeared on Fox Business News and other major media outlets.

Chris lives with her family in Vermont.

Learn more about Chris at www.chrisvanderzyden.com.

A Note From the Author

Entrepreneurship empowers women to take control of their own destiny in all parts of the world. I am particularly passionate about the positive impact that The BOMA Project has had upon the women in northern Kenya, as this population represents the poorest of the poor. 10% of net profits from this book will be donated to The BOMA Project to help expand their reach so that more women may reap the rewards of entrepreneurship. I thank you for purchasing this book to guide you in driving the success of your business, and for helping the women of northern Kenya reach their success.

~ Chris

"Our kids were starving. Now there is food to eat. No project has ever given us hope like this one. This is something that will stay. This is something within us."

(Holiya Eisimlesebe, BOMA business owner, Northern Kenya)

The BOMA Project is an innovative nonprofit that helps northern Kenyan women living in extreme poverty to become entrepreneurs in their rural villages. BOMA's Rural Entrepreneur Access Project (REAP) is a "poverty graduation" program that gives women a cash grant to launch a business, sustained training in business skills and savings, and two years of hands-on mentoring by local BOMA Village Mentors.

BOMA's success proves that the power of entrepreneurship is universal. In one of the poorest and most remote parts of the planet, women are using the basic building blocks of commerce—buying and selling, earning and saving, borrowing and lending—to transform their own lives. Women who used to be the village beggars, surviving on food aid and menial labor, are now hard-working and respected business owners. They are learning to read and write, sending their sons and daughters to school, breaking the cycle of poverty and dependency, and paving the way for a generation of change.

For more information, go to www.bomaproject.org.

Other Success Programs by Chris Vanderzyden

For more information go to
www.chrisvanderzyden.com

--- 7 Step VICTORY System™ Action Plan ---

How to Run Your Business at The Platinum Level

The Proven 7 Step VICTORY System™
to Elevate Your Business and Drive Profits

Success is not meant to be hard!

Never Before has there Been a Better Time to be Your Own Boss.

Take Action with the **7 Step VICTORY System™** for Entrepreneurs and Learn How To Develop a Successful Business that Produces the Highest Profits.

Clear Up the Confusion and Frustration of Selling in this Hyper-Competitive Digital Age.

The **7 Step VICTORY System™** for the Sales Professional will Keep Your Sales Cycle Full and Drive the Highest Profit Margin.

How To Drive Your Sales
To The Highest Level!

The proven
7 Step VICTORY System™
for keeping your sales
cycle full and producing
the highest PROFITS

Secrets to Growing Your Sales

A-Z BLUEPRINT FOR SUCCESS

Chris Vanderzyden

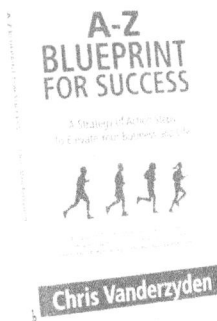

Elevate Your Business and Life with a Blueprint focused on Your Personal and Professional Development.

www.ingramcontent.com/pod-product-compliance
Lightning Source LLC
Chambersburg PA
CBHW060349220326
41598CB00023B/2854